PEOPLE
ON THE MOVE

AN ATLAS OF MIGRATION

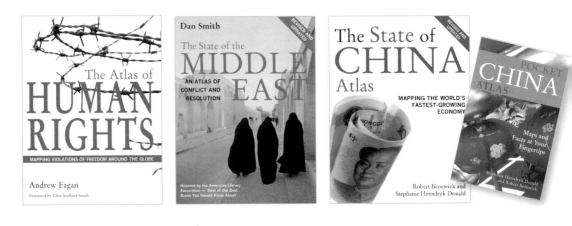

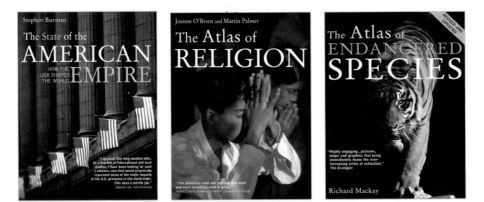

PEOPLE
ON THE MOVE

AN ATLAS OF MIGRATION

Russell King

Richard Black • Michael Collyer • Anthony Fielding • Ronald Skeldon

UNIVERSITY OF CALIFORNIA PRESS

Berkeley   Los Angeles

University of California Press, one of the most distinguished university presses in the United States, enriches lives around the world by advancing scholarship in the humanities, social sciences, and natural sciences. Its activities are supported by the UC Press Foundation and by philanthropic contributions from individuals and institutions. For more information, visit www.ucpress.edu.

University of California Press
Berkeley and Los Angeles, California

Library of Congress Control Number: 2010922173
ISBN: 0-520-26124-2 (cloth : alk. paper)
ISBN: 0-520-26151-8 (pbk. : alk. paper)

Produced for University of California Press by
Myriad Editions
Brighton, UK
www.MyriadEditions.com

Edited and co-ordinated by Jannet King and Candida Lacey
Designed by Isabelle Lewis and Corinne Pearlman
Maps and graphics created by Isabelle Lewis

Printed on paper produced from sustainable sources.
Printed and bound in Hong Kong through Lion Production
under the supervision of Bob Cassels, The Hanway Press, London.

15 14 13 12 11 10
10 9 8 7 6 5 4 3 2 1

CONTENTS

PART ONE

THE GRAND NARRATIVE:
MIGRATION THROUGH THE AGES   18

PART TWO

A WORLD IN FLUX:
CONTEMPORARY GLOBAL MIGRATION PATTERNS   38

Russell King is Professor of Geography at the University of Sussex, and Director of the Sussex Centre for Migration Research. He has been researching migration in its various forms around the world for over 30 years; his main research projects have been on Europe and the Mediterranean, including studies on Italian return migration, Irish migration, British retirement migration to Southern Europe, international student migration, migration and development in Albania, and Greek and Cypriot diasporas. He is the editor of the *Journal of Ethnic and Migration Studies*.

Richard Black is Professor of Human Geography at the University of Sussex, and Head of the School of Global Studies. His recent research has focused on the relationship between migration and poverty, but he has also conducted research on refugees, the integration of economic migrants from Eastern Europe in the UK, and the relationship between migration and climate change. His main geographical focus is Sub-Saharan Africa, but he has also carried out field research in Portugal, Greece and the Western Balkans. During 1994–2009 he was co-editor of the *Journal of Refugee Studies*.

Michael Collyer is Lecturer in Human Geography and Migration Studies at the University of Sussex. Whilst based at Sussex he has held a Nuffield Career Development Fellowship and a Marie Curie International Fellowship, with visiting appointments at universities in Morocco, Egypt and Sri Lanka. His research is on forced, undocumented and temporary forms of migration. He is an associate editor of the *Journal of Ethnic and Migration Studies*.

Tony Fielding is Research Professor in Human Geography at the University of Sussex, and has been researching migration for over 40 years. His main geographical focus is on Europe and East Asia, and he has been a visiting professor at Riksumeikan and Kyoto universities in Japan. His main research projects have been on counter-urbanization in Western Europe; the relationships between social and geographical mobility; theorizing new immigration trends in Southern Europe and East Asia; and, currently, the analysis of internal and international migration flows in China, Korea and Japan.

Ronald Skeldon is Professorial Fellow in the Department of Geography at the University of Sussex, and a Senior Research Fellow at the Department for International Development (DfID) in London. His research focuses on migration and development, and on both internal and international migrations. He has particular interests in the measurement of migration and in migration policy, and has acted as consultant to many international organizations. After early field research in Latin America, he has specialized in migration in Asia and the Pacific Region.

SUSSEX CENTRE FOR MIGRATION RESEARCH

The Sussex Centre for Migration Research (SCMR) is one of the UK's leading institutions for research on migration. Established in 1997 as a University of Sussex research centre of excellence, it brings together over 30 members of academic faculty from eight departments (geography, anthropology, economics, sociology, psychology, politics, international relations and development studies). The Centre runs the UK's only interdisciplinary doctoral programme in Migration Studies, as well as the UK's longest-running Masters programme in Migration Studies, which recruits students from around the world. It is led from the Department of Geography where, in the UK's Research Assessment Exercise in both 2001 and 2008, research on migration was flagged as being at the highest level, indicating research of consistent international excellence.

The Centre's research on migration is wide-ranging and explicitly international in its subject matter and audience. Current thematic research includes comparative studies on migration policy, migrant integration, and migration and development. Geographically, SCMR research has focused on the European Union, the Western Balkans, Sub-Saharan Africa, the Mediterranean, the Gulf and South Asia. Since 2003, SCMR has coordinated a major DfID-funded research network on migration and poverty, involving partners from a wide range of developing countries. It has also developed a major programme of research on diasporas, migration and identity, which has dealt with changing identities in countries of immigration (e.g. the UK) as well as the changing identities of migrants and returnees themselves (e.g. in Greece and Cyprus).

The Centre's research has received financial support from the UK's Economic and Social Research Council, the Arts and Humanities Research Council, the Nuffield Foundation, the Joseph Rowntree Foundation and the Leverhulme Trust. Staff from the Centre have also provided policy advice and commissioned research for a wide range of external organizations, including the United Nations, The World Bank, OECD, EU, Commonwealth, national and local government in the UK and development agencies such as Oxfam UK.

INTRODUCTION

Migration is a key issue of our times; indeed, it is sometimes said that we live in the "age of migration", referring, approximately, to the last 20 or so years. Today, there are more migrants on the move, their journeys more complex and uncertain than ever before. Migration seems to surround us all and to pervade all aspects of contemporary society. Now, and in the past, migration has provided millions with an escape route from poverty or oppression, ensuring the survival, even prosperity, of individuals and their families. New currents of human migration, triggered by economic need, ethnic cleansing or environmental catastrophe, are appearing all the time.

Definitions, concepts, numbers

At first glance, migration seems a straightforward concept: people move from one place or country to another and stay there long enough to be considered migrants. Behind this simplicity lies enormous variety and complexity – in spatial patterns, evolution through time, forms and types of movement, and causes and consequences. The study of migration is beset by dichotomies – forced vs. voluntary, temporary vs. permanent, legal vs. illegal, internal vs. international, skilled vs. unskilled, and many more. In practice, these dichotomies often become blurred. How to classify an individual driven to migrate by poverty and hunger, or a temporary migrant who continuously postpones return, or a legal migrant who becomes "illegal" through bureaucratic inability to renew a residence permit in time, or an internal migrant who then migrates internationally, or an Afghan doctor who drives a taxi in San Fransisco?

Above all, migration is a spatial event: it is about geographic distance, crossing borders, and movement and residence in different places. Therefore, it lends itself easily to mapping – either as "stocks", which are recorded at a particular moment in time such as by a census, or as "flows", which connect origins and destinations over a period of time such as a year or a decade.

We need to keep the question of numbers firmly in perspective. Ask people to estimate the number of migrants in the world (i.e. those born in one country, living in another), either as a global figure or as a fraction of the world's population, and they will probably give an estimate which is too high. The rhetoric of migration exaggerates its scale. We are told, in newspapers, by politicians, and even by academics who should know better, that "massive" numbers of people are on the move in the world today, that there is a "global migration crisis", and that migration is leading to a "clash of civilizations". This hype does enormous disservice to migrants who, already poor in many cases, are further vilified for their poverty and for trying to improve their lives through hard work in an unwelcoming environment where, furthermore, they are often scapegoated for the ills of the society they have joined.

According to the United Nations Population Division, there are 214 million international migrants in 2010, equivalent to 3 percent of the global population. This number has been growing steadily rather than exponentially: it was 175 million in 2000, 105 million in 1985, and 75 million in 1965. Percentage-wise it has grown much more slowly, from 2.3 percent of the world's population in 1965 to 3 percent today. This is because the world's population increases too, and migration only slightly tops that rate of growth.

However, all this ignores another fundamental component of the global migration map: internal migration. This is a much more difficult quantity to estimate. Countries vary enormously in size, and the definitions of how far an individual has to move to be recorded as a migrant will also vary. Usually, internal migration is recorded only when an administrative boundary is crossed, such as a province, thereby leaving out relocations within that unit. In 2009, the UN Population Division issued an estimate for total internal migrants in the world: 740 million. This is three and a half times the number of international migrants. Yet, when we think of migration, and even when scholars study migration, the focus is nearly always on international migrants.

The largest single migration in the world in recent years has been going on in China: more than 100 million people have relocated from the interior rural provinces to the burgeoning cities and industrial complexes of the coastal regions. All over the developing world, rural–urban migration drives urbanization. Most of the world's inhabitants now live in cities. Especially in Latin America, Asia, and Africa, rural poverty and increasing inequality pull millions of peasants out of the countryside towards overblown cities that are ill-equipped to receive them. Yet still they come.

Migration, then, takes many forms: people migrate as poor peasants, day labourers, industrial workers, skilled professionals, students, talented entrepreneurs; or as refugees and asylum seekers. They migrate alone, in families, or in large groups. Most are young adults, but many migrant flows, such as refugees, contain a substantial number of children and older people. People migrate for short or long periods. Or, like refugees, they may have no control over how long they are away; they may never be able to return, or they may be forced to return.

Another definitional problem thereby arises: how long does an individual have to be in the "other place" in order to be recognized as a migrant, as opposed to a visitor? There is no universally accepted answer to this question, although many statistical offices and censuses operate a one-year threshold. However this leaves out seasonal migration, which has always been a part of the migration picture – from the seasonal harvest migrants of medieval Europe to today's migrants who work seasonally in the tourism and construction industries. Hence the boundary between migration and mobility becomes blurred as seasonal, circular and cross-border shuttle migration becomes more widespread. Further blurring occurs on the tourism–migration boundary: for instance, migrants use tourist visas to enter a country and then overstay and become migrant workers; or "genuine" tourists, such as retirees, become long-stay visitors or residents.

Migration and the contradictions of globalization

Migration is one of the ironies of globalization. As enhanced mobility becomes a defining element of globalization, due to the falling cost of travel and ever-faster transport technologies, contradictory perspectives emerge. On the one hand, the increasing flows of migrant workers around the world are a direct result of the economic liberalism and multinational corporate enterprise that underpin globalization. On the other hand, while capital, goods, ideas and cultural influences are free to move around the world, sometimes instantaneously, people, that other key factor of production, are less free to migrate internationally than they were 50 or a 100 years ago.

As walls and fences come down, others go up, not just real ones (across the Mexico–US border, or separating off the Palestinian West Bank) but virtual ones in the form of surveillance, visa regimes and other restrictions on international movement. The New World Order that the collapse of the Soviet bloc promised has been a disillusionment, mired in post-communist ethnic wars, some of which have produced their own migration and refugee flows, as well as economic insecurity. The Iron Curtain, erected as a migration barrier by the communist regimes that came into power across Eastern Europe in the early post-war years, has been drawn back, only to be replaced by another barrier, which we can call an "ironic curtain", this time drawn shut by the West, which keeps out unwanted migrants from the East.

The globalization of the labour market thus sits in tension with states' wish to preserve their sovereignty and control over movement across their borders. Reduced to basics, the political economy of migration hinges on three elements: labour, capital and the state, each with their respective actors: migrants, employers, and politicians, and functionaries. Two opposing scenarios result from the interaction of these three elements – either a virtuous or a vicious triangle. The optimistic view sees employers and the receiving countries benefit from supplies of energetic foreign workers willing to take over unwanted jobs. The migrants get higher wages than they would have received at home, where they may well have been unemployed and destitute. Working and saving hard, they are able to transfer some of their wages as remittances to support family members back home, and stimulate the development of their communities and national economies by investment. The host society, meantime, is enriched by the cultural diversity that migrants bring. Everybody gains in this "quadruple-win" scenario – migrants, employers, the host country, and the sending country.

In the opposite interpretation, sending countries bemoan the loss of their most energetic and highly trained workers, whose education and upbringing have been paid for with scarce resources. Governments of the receiving countries see immigrants as causing unemployment for their nationals, incurring high welfare costs, and bringing cultural and ethnic conflict, even terrorism. Repeated use of terms such as "illegal immigrants" and "bogus asylum seekers" increases negative attitudes towards all immigrants. Xenophobia spreads and leads to racism, based on skin colour, religion or cultural difference, and the exercise of discrimination in many spheres of life.

In confronting the reality of international migration and the inexorable pressures driving it, states face many dilemmas. Countries like the USA and Canada have been built on immigration, which is therefore seen, historically, as a positive phenomenon and indeed as a fundamental part of national self-identity, even if in recent years there has been increasing selectivity in who is allowed in. European countries and Japan, on the other hand, have been less welcoming to immigrants, especially over the past 50 years. Here, we see a growing distinction, and contradiction, between intra-European migration, promoted as free movement within an enlarging European Union, and rigorous, often repressive, control over the entry of "third-country nationals" from outside the EU, and especially those coming from poor countries.

Migration has thus become central to domestic and international politics. As economic and social pressures to migrate increase, due above all to persisting and widening inequalities in the world, governments play cat and mouse with the migrants, a game that has both illogical and sometimes tragic consequences, especially in certain migration pressure points such as the Mexican–US border or the Strait of Gibraltar. Efforts by governments to regulate or to completely block migration only result in growing quantities of irregular or clandestine migration, the economic and human costs of which are overwhelmingly borne by the migrants themselves.

Policy dilemmas also confront the migrant-sending countries. Few want to be seen to be actively promoting emigration, regarded as a failure of the government to provide for the population's employment and well-being. The Philippines is one of the few countries that explicitly trains workers for "export". Plenty of others, however, give tacit approval to emigration, grateful for relieving the pressure on employment and resources, and even more thankful for the inflow of remittances. This inflow of hard-won foreign currency sustains sections of the population, helps to square fragile balance of payments, and is increasingly seen as a major factor for development – although the effectiveness of remittance-driven development is hotly debated.

Recently, the so-called "migration–development nexus" has been given global institutional recognition by the UN General Assembly's High Level Dialogue on International Migration and Development, launched in New York in 2006, and the Global Forum on Migration and Development, which has progressed via annual meetings in Brussels (2007), Manila (2008), and Athens (2009). There is a growing appreciation that migration holds considerable potential for economic and social development, and that this can best be achieved if migration is managed rather than just allowed to happen, if migrants are protected and empowered, and if migration is integrated with training and labour-market planning.

Russell King
February 2010

ACKNOWLEDGEMENTS

On behalf of the author team, I wish to thank a number of people who have been instrumental in the production of this Atlas. First, Candida Lacey of Myriad Editions, who convinced us from the outset that this was a worthwhile project – not that we needed much convincing! Second, Jannet King, whose meticulous eye for detail, and gentle, but necessarily persistent, chivvying are probably the main reasons why we kept to schedule. Third, Isabelle Lewis, whose design and cartography skills have helped to display visually, often for the first time, underlying patterns previously hidden within columns of data.

At Sussex we owe a particular debt of thanks to Adriana Castaldo for research assistance in gathering and processing data from various sources, and to Jenny Money for important liaison work. Thanks also to Anastasia Christou, Guita Hourani, Nayla Moukarbel, Tejinder Sandhu, Bao Shuming and Hye-jin Song for help in obtaining data for Greece, Lebanon, India, China, and Korea.

Russell King

Photo credits

Part One

THE GRAND NARRATIVE: MIGRATION THROUGH THE AGES

Our image of a sedentary world is seriously flawed: from time immemorial people have travelled, explored, relocated – indeed the roving instinct seems part of human nature. Migration is an ever-present theme in human history, although its significance has varied. Its scale has waxed and waned, whilst its causation and meaning exhibit many forms and linkages. It is bound up with a changing climate, the search for food, with conquest and colonialization, exploitation and suffering, freedom and liberation, banishment and exile. Migrants have been victims and heroes, marauding tyrants or just plain ordinary folk.

Controversy surrounds the exact chronology and routes taken by the first human migrants, as they moved out of their East African forests and gorges around 60,000 years ago. Carbon dating and new genetic evidence have created renewed speculation about this first, great migration, which is nothing less than the prehistoric peopling of the planet. Much, much later, around 10,000 years ago, in the riverine plains of the Middle East, hunter-gatherer survival gave way to settled agriculture and domestication of animals, followed, around 5,000 years ago, by irrigation and the foundation of towns and cities. Mobility changed. For the first time organized migrations were made possible by urban societies that grew ever more powerful.

Subsequently, we see not one historical grand narrative, but several. There is an ecological narrative, in which people move in search of food, cultivable land, pasture, water and other basic resources. Some societies are built around nomadism and transhumance, regular and seasonal circuits of movement. Young people grow up knowing they will leave their village because the soil is too poor or the climate too severe to sustain the population. But there is also a pioneering narrative, in which new (although rarely uninhabited) lands hold the promise of the freedom to expand and prosper. The great settlement migrations of the Han southwards through China from the 3rd to the 19th centuries, of Europeans to the Americas and Australia during the 19th and early 20th centuries, and of Russian peasants eastwards across Siberia at around the same time are obvious examples. Third, the Marxist narrative tells of exploitation, enslavement and indenture; of subject peoples bound by colonialism or greedy capitalism into the bondage of peripheral labour, until they are exhausted or die. And finally there is the diaspora narrative of exile and displacement from a homeland.

Dungeon in Elmira Castle, Ghana, once the largest slave-trading post in the world.

EARLY MIGRATIONS

The global distribution of humans is a result of thousands of years of migration.

The development of the modern human – *Homo sapiens* – and the dispersal of the species throughout the world is a matter of great debate and some controversy.

It is now generally accepted that *Homo sapiens* developed in Africa around 120,000 years ago, and started to move out of the continent around 60,000 years ago. The exact course of the migration, and point in time at which it occurred is still being pieced together – from archaeological evidence and, very recently, from a study of historical patterns in the genes of indigenous people worldwide. This map gives only a general idea of the likely sequence of the migration and of the time period.

Lascaux, France

Around 15,000 years ago, people created images on cave walls of the animals on which their lives depended.

Omo river valley, Ethiopia

This cranium of an early modern human, dating from 195,000 years ago, is known as Omo II.

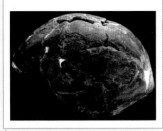

Northwest Australia

The Bradshaw Rock Paintings are thought to be among the first to depict clothing and ritual behaviour. They have been dated to at least 17,000 years ago or even older, although this is contested.

Human migration took place during the last ice age, when the climate was significantly different from that of today. For example, the Sahara desert was periodically covered in lush vegetation, whereas northern latitudes were regularly hidden under thick ice caps. With large amounts of water locked up in glaciers, the sea-level was much lower, exposing land-bridges between South-East Asia and Australia, and between Britain and northern Europe.

Exactly when the first modern humans made their way into North America is hotly disputed. Some archaeologists date it as recently as 10,000 to 15,000 years ago, but genetic evidence and recent finds suggest a somewhat earlier date.

Human tools

These fluted stone points are an example of many similar finds in North America that have been dated to around 13,000 years ago, and attributed to a people that archaeologists have named "Clovis", after the location of the first finds in the 1930s.

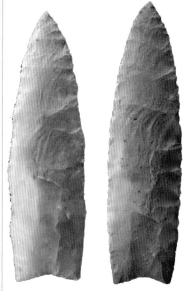

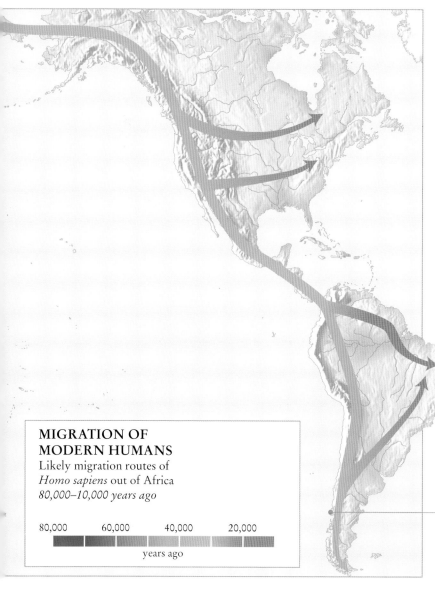

MIGRATION OF MODERN HUMANS

Likely migration routes of *Homo sapiens* out of Africa *80,000–10,000 years ago*

80,000	60,000	40,000	20,000

years ago

Monte Verde, Chile

Excavations at this site have uncovered evidence of human habitation dating from 14,000 to 15,000 years ago. As well as numerous artefacts, including spear points, scrapers and digging implements, the remains of meals, including mastodon and llama bones, fish, eggshells and seaweed, have also been found.

21

MEDITERRANEAN ODYSSEYS

During the Classical period, colonies not only provided trade and military security, but were a means of spreading the Greco-Roman culture and language.

While hunter-gatherers have always roved in search of greener pastures, the rise of urban civilizations based on agriculture changed the nature of migration. People settled in towns and cities as traders and administrators, and organized societies became capable of relocating large numbers of people through war, settlement and trade. Colonization – the deliberate, state-sponsored movement of peoples for political and economic purposes – was practised by the Greek city-states from the 8th century BCE, with established colonizer centres, such as Athens and Sparta, providing funds, organization and settlers.

The Ancient Greeks' colonizing migrations took place in two main waves. After the collapse of the Minoan and Mycenian civilizations on Crete and the southern Greek mainland, the Dorians moved outwards in all directions. They displaced the Ionians, who then moved further afield. The Phoenicians, a trading people with their homeland at the eastern end of the basin, also founded several important settlements, including Carthage in modern-day Tunisia.

Following the Punic Wars (264–146 BCE), which eclipsed the power of Carthage, Rome became the next hegemonic Mediterranean power. The entire basin was unified under a single administration, as were territories to the northwest, with Roman power extending from Hadrian's Wall in Britannia to the Nile Valley in Egypt. Migration underpinned the expansion of imperial power. Rome settled its newly conquered territories with army veterans and loyal migrants both from its heartland and other conquered regions, founding new colonies with local governments modelled on the Roman system.

Carthage, originally established as a trading town by the Phoenicians around 814 BCE, became a power in its own right but was vanquished by the Romans in 146 BCE at the end of the Punic Wars. The Romans destroyed the old city and built a new one, which included the Antonine Baths, shown here.

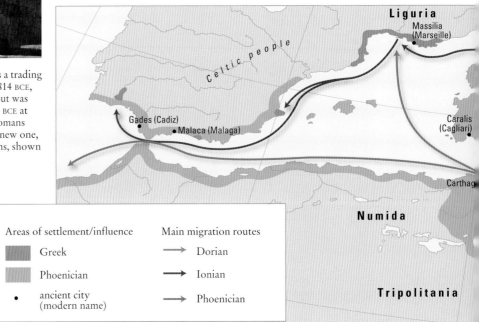

GREEK AND PHOENICIAN COLONIAL MIGRATIONS
1050–550 BCE

Areas of settlement/influence

■ Greek

■ Phoenician

• ancient city (modern name)

Main migration routes

→ Dorian

→ Ionian

→ Phoenician

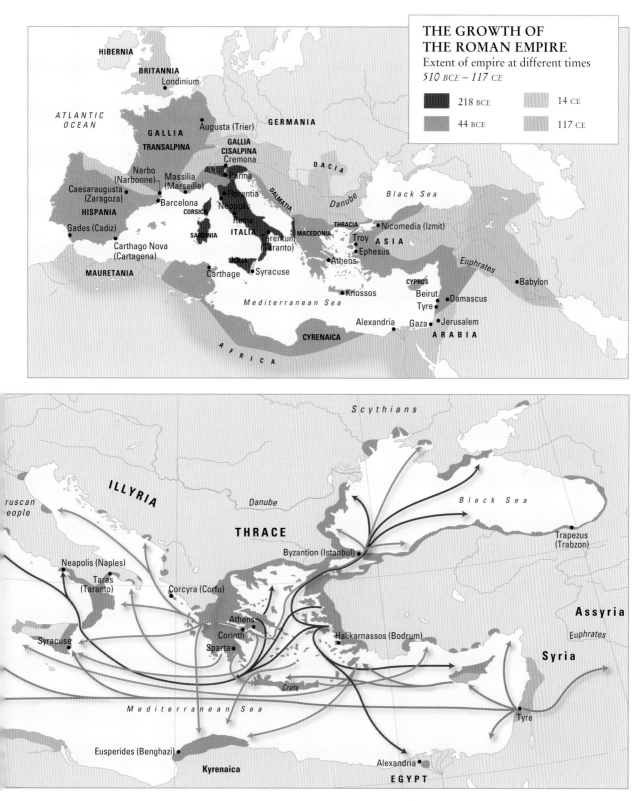

THE GROWTH OF THE ROMAN EMPIRE

Extent of empire at different times
510 BCE – 117 CE

- 218 BCE
- 44 BCE
- 14 CE
- 117 CE

Top map labels:

HIBERNIA
BRITANNIA
Londinium
ATLANTIC OCEAN
GALLIA TRANSALPINA
Augusta (Trier)
GERMANIA
GALLIA CISALPINA
Cremona
DACIA
Danube
Black Sea
Narbo (Narbonne)
Massilia (Marseille)
Parma
Florentia
DALMATIA
Caesaraugusta (Zaragoza)
Barcelona
CORSICA
Neapolis
Rome
ITALIA
HISPANIA
SARDINIA
Tarentum (Taranto)
MACEDONIA
THRACIA
Nicomedia (Izmit)
Troy
ASIA
Ephesus
Euphrates
Gades (Cadiz)
Carthago Nova (Cartagena)
SICILIA
Carthage
Syracuse
Athens
CYPRUS
Babylon
MAURETANIA
Knossos
Beirut
Damascus
Tyre
Mediterranean Sea
Alexandria
Gaza
Jerusalem
CYRENAICA
ARABIA
AFRICA

Bottom map labels:

Scythians
ILLYRIA
Danube
Black Sea
ruscan eople
THRACE
Byzantion (Istanbul)
Trapezus (Trabzon)
Neapolis (Naples)
Taras (Taranto)
Corcyra (Corfu)
Assyria
Athens
Euphrates
Corinth
Halikarnassos (Bodrum)
Syria
Sparta
Syracuse
Crete
Mediterranean Sea
Tyre
Eusperides (Benghazi)
Kyrenaica
Alexandria
EGYPT

SLAVE MIGRATIONS

The transatlantic slave trade was the largest ever forced migration.

Enslavement is an old practice. Throughout the Ancient World of Egypt, Greece and Rome, slaves were transported for labour in quarries, agriculture and public construction projects. However, it was the transatlantic slave trade that contributed the largest, as well as the most brutal and tragic, forced migration the world has ever seen. During four centuries – from the start of the 16th to the end of the 19th – around 11 million Africans were taken as slaves to North and South America and the Caribbean, 84 percent of them between 1700 and 1850.

Slave migrations were a fundamental component of commodity production for the European colonial system, and part of the "triangular trade". Ships set out from European ports carrying arms, manufactured goods and alcohol; these were traded with African chiefs for slaves, who were marshalled at fortified collecting points along the West African coast between the Senegal River and Luanda. The slaves were transported across the Atlantic, on what was called the "middle passage", in conditions of indescribable filth and cruelty that killed, on average, one in seven. They were then sold and put to work in mines and plantations producing gold, sugar ("brown gold"), coffee, cotton and tobacco. These lucrative goods were transported on the third leg of the triangle to Europe. Ill-treatment and remorselessly tough working regimes meant that around a third of slaves died within the first few years of arrival.

Transatlantic slavery was pioneered by the Spanish and Portuguese. The virtual annihilation by the Spanish colonists of the indigenous people whom they had been using as their labour force led to the import of African slaves as early as the 16th century. The Portuguese were already transporting slaves to Lisbon as house-servants and to their Atlantic island colonies (São Tomé, Cape Verde, Madeira, and the Azores) for agricultural labour. Their territories in north-east Brazil eventually became one vast sugar plantation, absorbing more than 3.5 million slaves until slavery was abolished there in 1888.

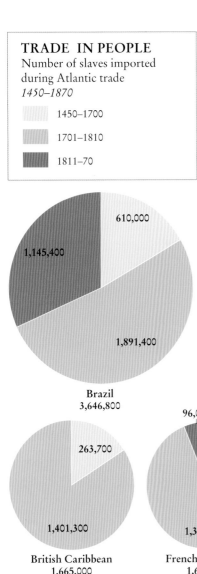

TRADE IN PEOPLE
Number of slaves imported during Atlantic trade
1450–1870

- 1450–1700
- 1701–1810
- 1811–70

Brazil
3,646,800

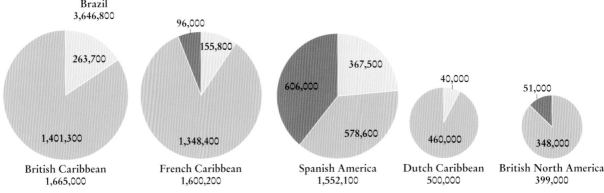

British Caribbean
1,665,000

French Caribbean
1,600,200

Spanish America
1,552,100

Dutch Caribbean
500,000

British North America
399,000

The Caribbean, meanwhile, became the domain of British, French, and Dutch colonial slavery. Each Caribbean island typically housed a small population of white residents and a large number of slaves. In the 1830s, for instance, Jamaica had 20,000 whites and 310,000 slaves; Martinique 9,000 and 78,000. Moving north, the "slave states" of the southern USA – Virginia, North and South Carolina, Georgia, Mississippi, Alabama, Louisiana – were home to extensive tobacco and cotton plantations, but slaves also worked in coalmines, forestry and railway construction. Later, after abolition in 1865, they would migrate north to the industrial powerhouses of the northern USA.

African slaves not only went west. An earlier-established, and longer-lasting, transport of slaves – between 4 million and 5 million overall – took place northwards across the Sahara and along the East Coast to the Persian Gulf, the Red Sea, and the Arab and Ottoman empires.

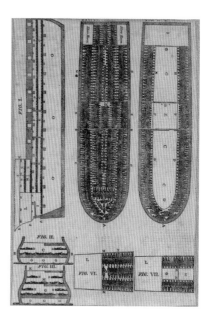

On the transatlantic voyage, men, women and children were packed tightly below decks in appalling conditions.

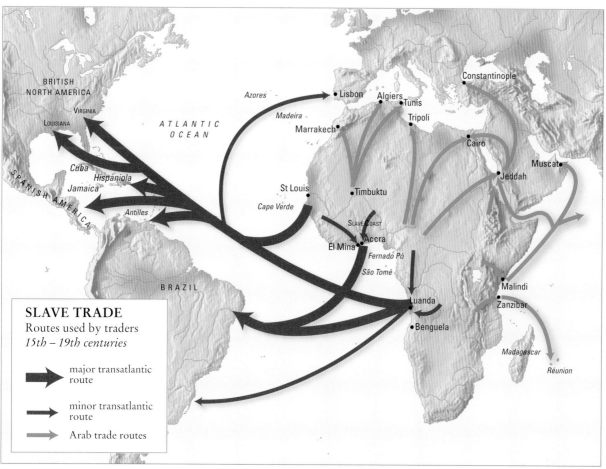

SLAVE TRADE
Routes used by traders
15th – 19th centuries

➤ major transatlantic route

→ minor transatlantic route

→ Arab trade routes

MIGRATIONS OF INDENTURE

The system of indentured labour provided cheap, easily exploited, workers who were shipped in large numbers mainly to European colonies.

The abolition of slavery during the 19th century removed a ready source of extremely low-cost labour for colonial administrators and plantation-owners, despite the willingness of some freed slaves to be re-employed as waged workers. The scarcity of cheap labour was solved by a new form of exploitative, globe-spanning migration: indentured labour. This enabled the European colonial powers and plantation owners to plunder the vast labour reserves in Asia. The migrants, mostly Indian and Chinese, were taken to the old plantation colonies of the Caribbean, and to colonial societies that had not benefited from African slave labour. Over 60,000 Pacific Islanders were also taken (sometimes forcibly) to work in Queensland, Australia between 1863 and 1904, although most eventually returned home.

Indentured labourers were taken on as paid workers, on a contract that usually lasted for one or more years, and normally included the passage home. However, they were bound by strict rules that were often abused by employers and agents. This could lead to the workers

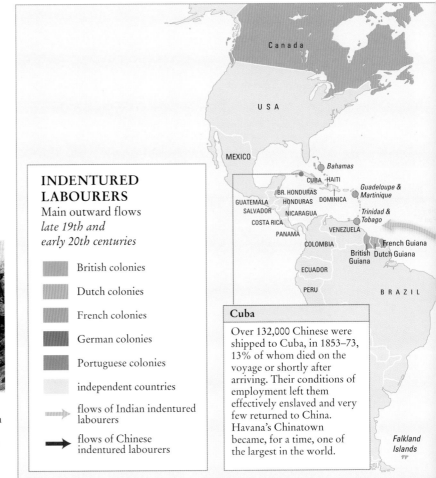

INDENTURED LABOURERS
Main outward flows
late 19th and early 20th centuries

- British colonies
- Dutch colonies
- French colonies
- German colonies
- Portuguese colonies
- independent countries
- flows of Indian indentured labourers
- flows of Chinese indentured labourers

Cuba

Over 132,000 Chinese were shipped to Cuba, in 1853–73, 13% of whom died on the voyage or shortly after arriving. Their conditions of employment left them effectively enslaved and very few returned to China. Havana's Chinatown became, for a time, one of the largest in the world.

Uganda Railway
Between 1896 and 1901, indentured Indian labourers were used to build a railway between Mombasa, on the coast of British East Africa, and Lake Victoria, thereby improving access to Uganda.

becoming indebted and in a position where they could either not return, or returned broke, and often in poor health. In effect, this new system of slavery was little better than the one it replaced.

The geography of indenture migrations is complex. Many countries were involved and the data are fragmentary. Difficulties surround the exact definition of indenture and its blurring of the distinction between forced and voluntary migration. Much of the movement was short-term, unlike slave migration. Around 30 million indentured workers emigrated from India in the 100 years following the 1830s, and 24 million returned. Both the number emigrating and the rate of return were higher for China, but fewer females were involved. Both India and China saw a net migration of between 5 million and 7 million people.

Indenture epitomized the colonial principle of divide and rule, pitting one subservient and exploited population against another. Like slavery before it, indenture migration contributed to both the racial stratification and the cultural plurality of many countries and cities.

Chinese syndicates
Syndicates based in China and San Francisco were responsible for a large number of indentured labourers, including 50,000 sent to work in the California gold mines in the early 1850s. Labourers were taken, some of them forcibly, from southern China, via the ports of Hong Kong, Macau and Shanghai.

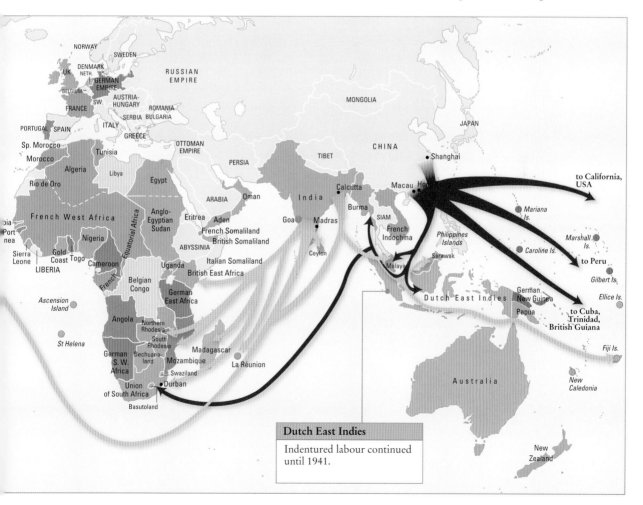

Dutch East Indies

Indentured labour continued until 1941.

THE GREAT MIGRATION

More than 50 million people emigrated from Europe to the USA during the 19th and early 20th centuries in the largest ever international free movement of people.

The Statue of Liberty – for millions of migrants their first sight, and iconic symbol, of the USA – bears the words: "Give me your tired, your poor, your huddled masses yearning to be free."

The mass relocation known as "the Great Migration" was caused by a number of factors. Migrants were driven out of Europe by poverty, unemployment and the desire to start a new life, and were drawn by the opportunities, space and freedom offered by the Americas. Although the dreams of those who ended up as itinerant labourers or overworked factory hands may have faded to disillusionment, many did become prosperous farmers, successful craftsmen, business owners, or white-collar workers. Others at least saw their children and grandchildren achieve education and upward social mobility.

There was a clear distinction between the "old" and "new" migrations. The first predominated during much of the 19th century, and involved family groups from the UK, Ireland, Germany, and Scandinavia seeking permanent settlement. The second developed in the late 19th century and lasted until the First World War, involved people from Poland, Austria-Hungary, Italy, and the Balkan states, and was initially characterized by the temporary movement of single men.

Behind these general patterns lies significant variation. Norway's population explosion and its failure to industrialize led to a high proportion of its population emigrating. In neighbouring Sweden, however, where industrial and urban growth were more evident, a much smaller proportion emigrated.

Many early arrivals in the USA assimilated quickly, but the reaction to the entry in the 1840s of 1 million or more Catholic Irish fleeing the potato famine made immigration more of a social and political issue. Eventually, the Irish were allowed to make America their home, as were successive waves of migrants – Jews from Russia, peasants from Italy, and Chinese entering via America's Pacific coast. International migrations triggered major population movements within the USA: the epic westward journeys of the wagon trains and the Gold Rush to California, and the northward migration of African-Americans leaving racial persecution in the rural south to seek work in the industrial north.

EUROPEAN EMIGRATION
Number of emigrants per 10,000 population
1861–1910

■	more than 80
▦	61 – 80
▨	41 – 60
▨	21 – 40
▧	fewer than 20
▧	no data

1861–70

Finland (RUSSIAN EMPIRE)
NORWAY
Scotland
SWEDEN
DENMARK
England
NETHS
Ireland
BELGIUM
GERMAN EMPIRE
FRANCE   SWITZ.
AUSTRO-HUNGARIAN EMPIRE
ITALY
PORTUGAL   SPAIN

1871–80

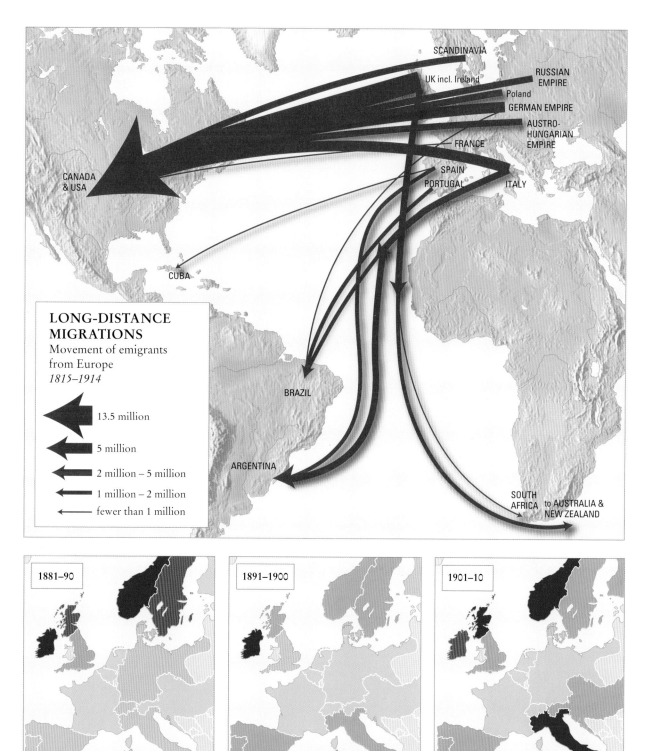

SCANDINAVIA

UK incl. Ireland

RUSSIAN EMPIRE

Poland

GERMAN EMPIRE

AUSTRO-HUNGARIAN EMPIRE

FRANCE

SPAIN
PORTUGAL

ITALY

CANADA & USA

CUBA

LONG-DISTANCE MIGRATIONS
Movement of emigrants from Europe
1815–1914

13.5 million

5 million

2 million – 5 million

1 million – 2 million

fewer than 1 million

BRAZIL

ARGENTINA

SOUTH AFRICA

to AUSTRALIA & NEW ZEALAND

1881–90

1891–1900

1901–10

30–31 Migration from Italy; 32–33 Nation-Building Migrations ▶▶ **29**

MIGRATION FROM ITALY

The poorest people are usually not the first to migrate from a poor country.

Italy is one of the classic countries of emigration. Between the 1870s and the 1970s, around 26 million people left the country, not only to travel across the Atlantic but also to other European countries, Australia and South Africa.

The geography of Italian emigration to the Americas illustrates an important and recurrent feature of the phenomenon of migration: when a migration flow develops from a poor country, the first to leave are usually the relatively well-off, who have the knowledge and contacts to move. Only later does "emigration fever" spread to poorer, more remote parts of the country.

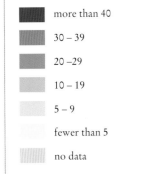

RATE OF EMIGRATION
Annual number of emigrants per 1,000 population
1880–1915

- more than 40
- 30 – 39
- 20 – 29
- 10 – 19
- 5 – 9
- fewer than 5
- no data

From the 1890s onwards, Italy became the major source of migrants to both North and South America. Between 1880 and 1914, 4.1 million people migrated from Italy to the USA, a further 1.8 million to Argentina and 1.2 million to Brazil.

Northern Italians dominated the early decades of the exodus, and Southerners took over after the turn of the 20th century. In the early years especially, the majority of Northern Italians went to South America, but some did go to North America. Southern Italians went mainly to North America, with relatively few heading for South America.

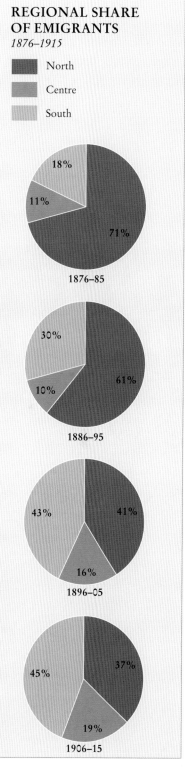

REGIONAL SHARE OF EMIGRANTS
1876–1915

- North
- Centre
- South

18% 11% 71%
1876–85

30% 10% 61%
1886–95

43% 16% 41%
1896–05

45% 19% 37%
1906–15

NATION-BUILDING MIGRATIONS

Some migrations are encouraged and planned by governments to increase the land under state control.

Some migrations are of lasting significance, not just because of the number of people involved, but for the impact they have on the existing inhabitants. Many of these are "pioneer migrations" – movements of people that take place as a result of government policy, financial inducements, and maybe even military support.

Ostensibly aimed at opening up new lands to cultivation, pioneer migrations are equally about nation-building and bringing land more securely under central state control. They have taken place at different times and in different regions of the world. The classic pioneer migrations were those westwards across North America in the 18th and 19th centuries, which essentially created the modern USA in both reality and myth. In the process, however, this influx of European American farmers displaced the Native American inhabitants, many of whom were forced westwards, and most of whom ended up restricted to reservations.

Pioneer migrations tend to work against the more usual rural-to-urban migrations, and often send out people from densely populated towns, cities and farmland to more sparsely populated areas. More recent attempts to consolidate the nation through pioneer migrations can be seen in the expansion of agricultural communities in the Amazon basin by the independent states of South America, whose populations are largely concentrated in coastal or mountain environments. Vast interior areas of resource-rich, sparsely populated lands were settled, especially during the second half of the 20th century. By increasing the areas under production, the settlement programmes extended the area under state control, often including territory considered at risk of occupation by rival states.

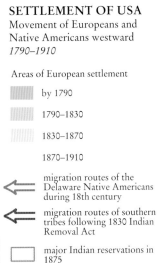

Initially on foot or on horseback, the great westward migrations were later facilitated by the expansion of the railways

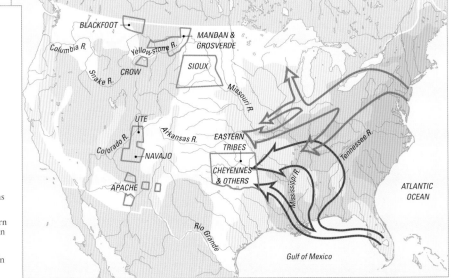

SETTLEMENT OF USA
Movement of Europeans and Native Americans westward
1790–1910

Areas of European settlement

- by 1790
- 1790–1830
- 1830–1870
- 1870–1910

⬅ migration routes of the Delaware Native Americans during 18th century

⬅ migration routes of southern tribes following 1830 Indian Removal Act

▭ major Indian reservations in 1875

BLACKFOOT
Columbia R.
Yellowstone R.
MANDAN & GROSVERDE
CROW
SIOUX
Snake R.
Missouri R.
UTE
Arkansas R.
EASTERN TRIBES
Colorado R.
NAVAJO
CHEYENNES & OTHERS
APACHE
Mississippi R.
Tennessee R.
ATLANTIC OCEAN
Rio Grande
Gulf of Mexico

In China, there has been state-sponsored movement of Han Chinese into Tibet and Xinjiang in recent years. By putting Han Chinese into powerful party and state positions, the state government has brought these minority-ethnic western provinces under more effective control.

In Indonesia, the transmigration programmes had moved more than 6 million people from the densely populated islands of Java and Bali to the outer islands by 1999, although the migration has decreased significantly in recent years. Both rural and urban settlements were established, but these have led to conflicts between local populations and Javanese settlers, including the successful war of independence waged by the East Timorese. Of greater significance for the global climate is the destruction of tropical forests and the expansion of populations into semi-arid environments.

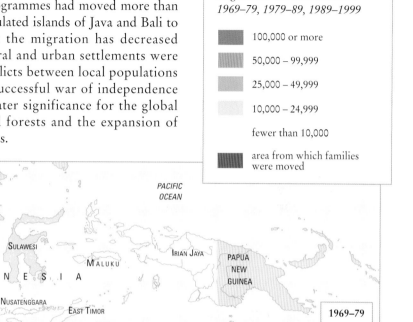

PLANNED MIGRATION
Number of families moved into area in series of planned migrations within Indonesia
1969–79, 1979–89, 1989–1999

100,000 or more

50,000 – 99,999

25,000 – 49,999

10,000 – 24,999

fewer than 10,000

area from which families were moved

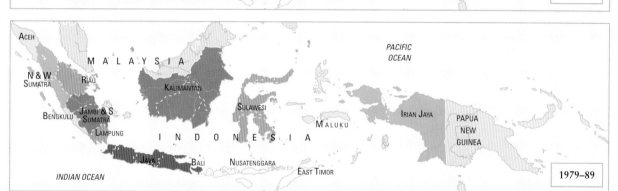

COLONIAL MIGRATIONS

Colonization by Europeans resulted in the movement of millions of people, and had a major impact on populations around the world.

At least 500 years of colonialism by European powers resulted in the movement of millions of people, and had a huge impact on the ethnic make-up of countries as far apart as Peru and Australia. The maximum extent of the European empires was reached at different historical points. The Spanish empire largely disintegrated from 1810 onwards, while that of the British and French expanded after the First World War with the redistribution of German territories.

The lasting impact on the populations of colonized territories varied widely. British colonial policy encouraged its citizens to achieve territorial domination in colonized countries by settling there, but to develop separate institutional and cultural activities from those of the indigenous people. By contrast, Spanish colonization involved relations between male military personnel and indigenous women that led to a predominantly creolized culture in most of Latin America, although the proportion of the population that is *mestizo* (Amerindian-Spanish) now varies widely between countries.

Dutch colonialism was founded less on settlement and more on commercial objectives, while the Portuguese migrated widely beyond their colonial territories. French colonization resembled that of the

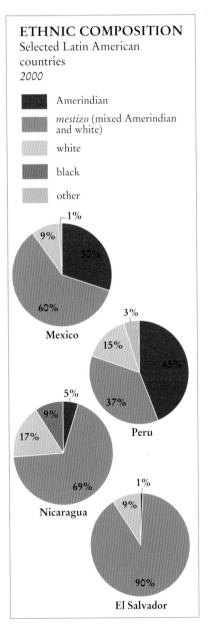

ETHNIC COMPOSITION
Selected Latin American countries
2000

- Amerindian
- *mestizo* (mixed Amerindian and white)
- white
- black
- other

Mexico
1% · 9% · 30% · 60%

Peru
3% · 15% · 45% · 37%

Nicaragua
5% · 9% · 17% · 69%

El Salvador
1% · 9% · 90%

EUROPEAN EMPIRES
1914

- British colonies
- Dutch colonies
- French colonies
- German colonies
- Portuguese colonies
- ▪ ex-Portuguese colony
- ▪ territory in Latin America previously part of the Spanish Empire
- independent countries

Movement of Europeans to colonies *since 1500:*

- ➡ British
- ➡ Dutch
- ➡ French
- ➡ Portuguese
- ➡ Spanish

Canada · 2.5 million

USA

MEXICO · Bahamas · CUBA · HAITI · BR. HONDURAS · HONDURAS · DOMINICA · Guadeloupe & Martinique · GUATEMALA · SALVADOR · NICARAGUA · Trinidad & Tobago · COSTA RICA · VENEZUELA · PANAMA · COLOMBIA · French Guiana · British Dutch Guiana · Guiana · ECUADOR · PERU · BRAZIL

to Latin America: 550,000 · 1,000

Falkland Islands

British, which can at least partly be explained by the direct competition between them.

The end of European empires provoked further migrations, this time back to Europe. On the independence of Algeria in 1962, an estimated 900,000 European colonists (known as *pieds noirs*) were allowed into France, though many were not of French origin. Military withdrawal from Portugal's African colonies between 1974 and 1979 led to an estimated 800,000 people of Portuguese origin migrating to Portugal. Around 300,000 Dutch Indonesians migrated to the Netherlands between 1950 and 1958. Although many "returnees" had never actually been to their country of citizenship, they were mostly accepted with enthusiasm by its government and people. However, when Idi Amin's regime in Uganda expelled all Asians in 1972, fewer than half were accepted by the British government.

The end of empires also resulted in other sorts of migration – those of the indigenous people. The most dramatic was that of the Hindus and Muslims, which took place as a result of the partition of British India in 1947, and which further exacerbated the lasting damage caused by European colonialism.

Partition of India
The partition of British India in August 1947 into modern India, West Pakistan and East Pakistan (which became Bangladesh in 1971) led to 14.5 million Muslims and Hindus crossing the new international borders.

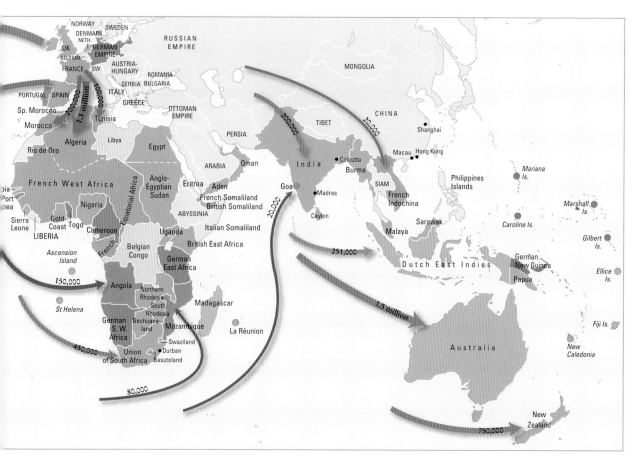

DIASPORAS

Many modern diasporas are not forced exiles, but are driven by trade or work.

Three core criteria help to define a diaspora: dispersion across international space, orientation to a homeland, and a clear sense of common identity sustained through ethnicity, language, and religion.

Inscribed into the traditional definition of diaspora (from the Greek for "scattering") is the notion of forced exile as a result of persecution, such as occurred in the classic diasporas of the Jews, Armenians, Palestinians, and Kurds. In recent decades, other diasporas have been recognized: colonial diasporas, such as those of the British and Portuguese; trading diasporas, such as that of the Lebanese; and labour migration diasporas, such as those of Indian indentured workers in the 19th century or Caribbean workers over the last 50 years.

Some diasporas, such as those of the Greek or Chinese, incorporate more than one type, either simultaneously or at different times. Others stand outside some of the conventional criteria. For instance, African-Americans, descendants of the slave diaspora, can no longer precisely locate their homeland. New diasporas are formed or invented as a result of political change or economic challenges, for example in Africa, where governments try to mobilize the development potential of the diaspora through encouragement to invest or return.

The three maps show contrasting diaspora situations. The contemporary distribution of the Jews reflects over two millennia of exile and "rediasporization", as well as "return" to Israel. The modern Lebanese diaspora maps the geography of its trading settlements over the past 100 years. And the current distribution of Greeks comprises a mixture of early colonies, trading settlements in Africa, and labour migration to North America, Australia, and Germany.

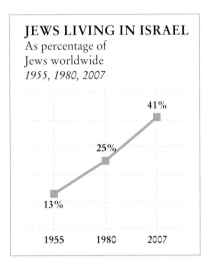

JEWS LIVING IN ISRAEL
As percentage of Jews worldwide
1955, 1980, 2007

41%
25%
13%

1955   1980   2007

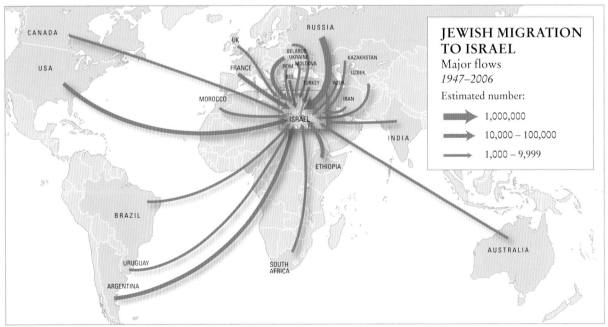

JEWISH MIGRATION TO ISRAEL
Major flows
1947–2006
Estimated number:
→ 1,000,000
→ 10,000 – 100,000
→ 1,000 – 9,999

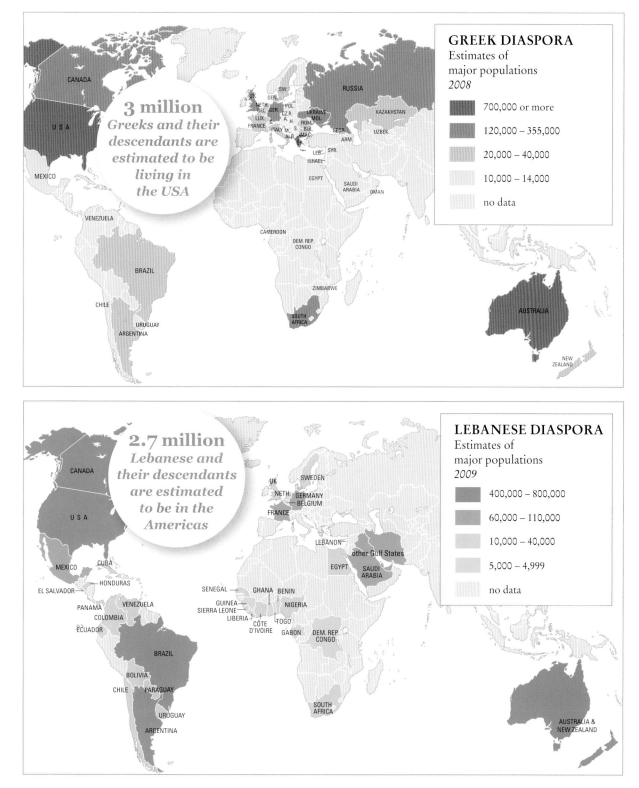

GREEK DIASPORA
Estimates of
major populations
2008

- 700,000 or more
- 120,000 – 355,000
- 20,000 – 40,000
- 10,000 – 14,000
- no data

3 million
Greeks and their descendants are estimated to be living in the USA

CANADA
USA
MEXICO
VENEZUELA
BRAZIL
CHILE
URUGUAY
ARGENTINA
UK
NETH.
BEL.
LUX.
FRANCE
SW.
DEN.
GER.
POL.
CZ.R.
A.
H.
ITALY M.
S.
ALB.
GR.
MAC.
BUL.
ROM.
MOL.
UKRAINE
GEOR.
ARM.
RUSSIA
KAZAKHSTAN
UZBEK.
LEB.
ISRAEL
SYR.
EGYPT
SAUDI
ARABIA
OMAN
CAMEROON
DEM. REP.
CONGO
ZIMBABWE
SOUTH
AFRICA
AUSTRALIA
NEW
ZEALAND

LEBANESE DIASPORA
Estimates of
major populations
2009

- 400,000 – 800,000
- 60,000 – 110,000
- 10,000 – 40,000
- 5,000 – 4,999
- no data

2.7 million
Lebanese and their descendants are estimated to be in the Americas

CANADA
USA
MEXICO
CUBA
HONDURAS
EL SALVADOR
PANAMA
COLOMBIA
ECUADOR
VENEZUELA
BRAZIL
BOLIVIA
CHILE
PARAGUAY
URUGUAY
ARGENTINA
UK
NETH.
FRANCE
SWEDEN
GERMANY
BELGIUM
LEBANON
other Gulf States
EGYPT
SAUDI
ARABIA
SENEGAL
GUINEA
SIERRA LEONE
LIBERIA
GHANA
CÔTE
D'IVOIRE
TOGO
BENIN
NIGERIA
GABON
DEM. REP.
CONGO
SOUTH
AFRICA
AUSTRALIA &
NEW ZEALAND

37

Part Two

A WORLD IN FLUX: CONTEMPORARY GLOBAL MIGRATION PATTERNS

The maps examining the evolution of global migration since the Second World War vary in scale and purpose, ranging from global through regional to national. What drives most of the migrations discussed is geographical inequality: people are migrating, both internationally and internally, in the hope of improving their lives through access to better-paid and more secure work.

The link between labour migration and industrial development was never more clear than in Western Europe and North America in the decades following the war. Migrant workers seemed intrinsic to this kind of "Fordist" production, based on assembly lines and abundant, docile labour. Regional migration systems linked industrial "cores" with migrant "peripheries": Western Europe with its Mediterranean Basin migrant-source countries; the USA with its migrant satellites in Central America, the Caribbean with the states of its own Deep South. Later, the oil-rich Gulf fashioned its constellation of poor labour-supply countries in South Asia and beyond, and recently Russia's industries and oil and gas fields have drawn in migrant workers from a broad range of sources, including post-Soviet successor states such as Ukraine and Uzbekistan, the Russian Far East, and China.

Migration patterns change. Particularly in the wake of the 1970s oil crisis, new dynamics unfolded. Some migrant workers returned to their home countries; rather more stayed on, reuniting their families in a "quiet migration" that transformed "guest-workers" into settled minority ethnic communities. Southern Europe, newly incorporated into the European Community, and riding a "post-Fordist" wave based not on industrial production but on tourism and services, turned from a region of emigration to one of immigration. Many migrations remained regionalized, for instance across the Mediterranean, but others became globalized, as Latin Americans moved to Europe as well as the USA, or Africans migrated to North America as well as to Europe.

The contemporary era is also one of accelerating internal migration, the scale of which, especially in large countries such as the USA, India, and China, far exceeds international moves. In the last two countries, and in the rest of the less developed world, migration, abroad and, more commonly, to urban and industrial centres within the country, can be a route out of poverty – a means of survival and ultimately, for some, a step to a measure of prosperity.

One of China's 132 million rural migrant workers arriving in Xiamen.

GLOBAL MIGRATION

Globally, 3 percent of people are international migrants, but the share varies enormously from one country to another.

In 2010, there were a total of 214 million international migrants – people living in a country other than that of their birth – which equates to 3 percent of the world's population. To some extent, this belies the enormous political significance that migration seems to have in countries keen to control or even to ban immigration. In fact, the share of the world's population who are international migrants has been increasing only fractionally over several decades, due to the pace of overall population growth. In 2000, there were 175 million international migrants, representing 2.9 percent of global population. Back in 1965, the figures were 75 million and 2.3 percent.

Although the most important direction of flow is from the less to the more developed countries, there are also substantial flows between highly developed countries (especially within Europe and amongst other OECD countries), and almost equally large flows between less developed countries (notably within Latin America, within Asia and

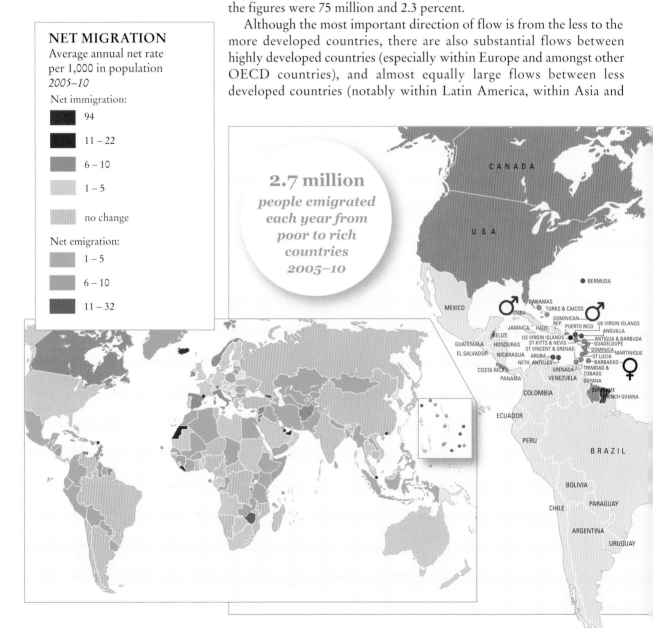

NET MIGRATION
Average annual net rate per 1,000 in population
2005–10

Net immigration:

94

11 – 22

6 – 10

1 – 5

no change

Net emigration:

1 – 5

6 – 10

11 – 32

2.7 million
people emigrated each year from poor to rich countries 2005–10

within Africa). On the whole, poor countries (but not necessarily the poorest) are sources of emigration; wealthy countries receive migrants, not always willingly. In most immigration countries in Europe, North America and Australasia, immigrants represent between 5 percent and 24 percent of the population. However, in the Gulf States it is much higher, reaching 87 percent in Qatar.

Globally, 49 percent of international migrants are females, and many flows – both emigrants and immigrants – are at approximate parity. However, females tend to be the majority in several European countries, whilst males are more numerous in several oil-producing Middle Eastern countries. The differences in sex ratios are explained by the interaction of three factors: the nature of the labour-market opportunities in the destination countries, the openness to family migration and long-term settlement, and the cultural and religious norms of both the sending and the host countries

MIGRANTS
As percentage of total population
2010

- 50% or more
- 25% – 49%
- 5% – 24%
- fewer than 5%
- no data

♀ 58% or more of migrants are female

♂ 58% or more of migrants are male

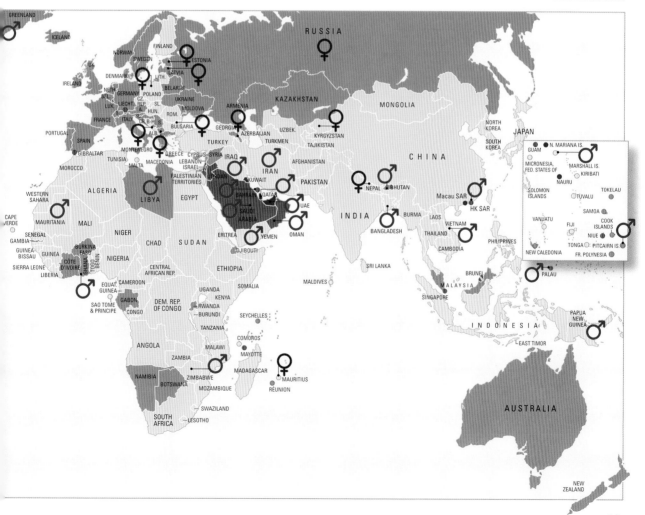

POST-WAR MIGRATION OF WORKERS

The post-war economic boom led to a flow of migrant manual workers, often managed through governmental bilateral agreements.

The period of immense growth in the industrial world from the late 1940s to the early 1970s was largely based on the mass production of standardized goods for mass markets. Such "Fordist" industrial development needed vast numbers of workers to produce the goods, and then to spend their rising wages on buying them. Initially, local workers were employed, but as more people were needed, workers were recruited both from the rural peripheries of the industrialized countries and from non-industrialized countries – typically from near neighbours. These migration flows consisted primarily of young single adult men with few or no qualifications. They did the most monotonous and routine production jobs, and the hard physical work needed to construct the new urban infrastructure and suburban development that typifies this period.

This form of international migration in Europe was managed to a significant degree through bilateral agreements between the sending and receiving countries. The migrants were subjected to a selection process to ensure that they were strong and healthy, and were given only short-term contracts. They were seen as temporary "guest-workers", not as permanent settlers. To the employers, they were a kind of reserve army of labour – one they could draw upon when times were good but send back when times were bad.

Somewhat to the surprise of governments, a high proportion of migrants stayed, married, raised families, and became permanent residents and, eventually, citizens of the countries to which they had migrated. Hence, to take just two examples, the strong presence of Italian, Yugoslav, Greek and Turkish immigrant minorities in Germany, and of North African and Portuguese immigrant minorities in France.

In Japan, there were particularly high rates of population growth around Tokyo and Osaka, and also around Nagoya, which was then the centre of the Japanese car industry.

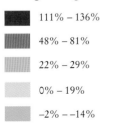

POPULATION MOVEMENTS IN JAPAN
Percentage change in population of prefectures *1948–70*

Average change: 30% increase

- 111% – 136%
- 48% – 81%
- 22% – 29%
- 0% – 19%
- –2% – –14%

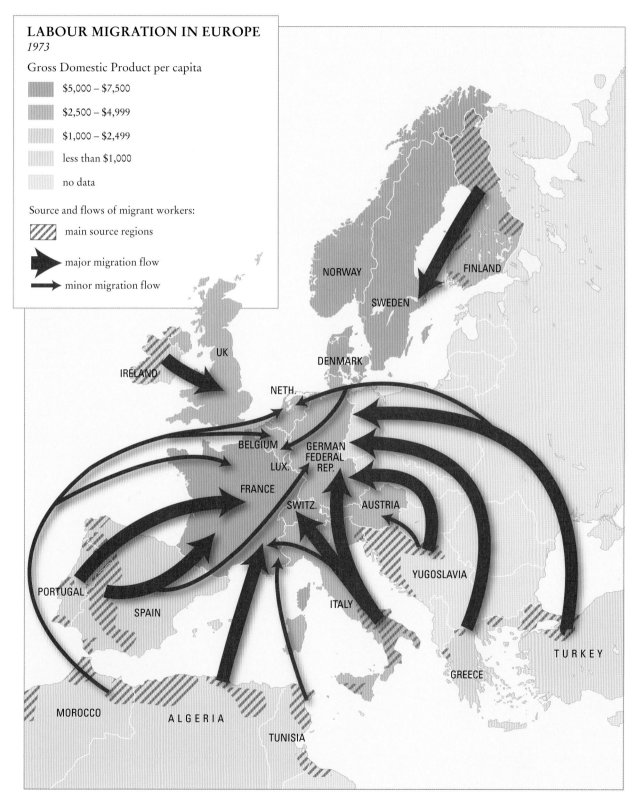

LABOUR MIGRATION IN EUROPE
1973

Gross Domestic Product per capita

- $5,000 – $7,500
- $2,500 – $4,999
- $1,000 – $2,499
- less than $1,000
- no data

Source and flows of migrant workers:

- main source regions
- major migration flow
- minor migration flow

NORWAY
FINLAND
SWEDEN
UK
DENMARK
IRELAND
NETH.
BELGIUM
GERMAN FEDERAL REP.
LUX.
FRANCE
SWITZ.
AUSTRIA
YUGOSLAVIA
PORTUGAL
SPAIN
ITALY
MOROCCO
ALGERIA
TUNISIA
GREECE
TURKEY

NEW WORKER MIGRATIONS

Since the 1980s, migrants from diverse countries have made southern Europe their destination.

MIGRANT POPULATIONS IN PORTUGAL
Regional distribution of main immigrant populations
2008

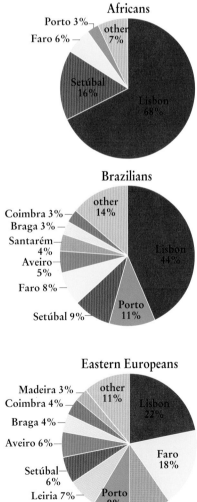

Africans
- Porto 3%
- Faro 6%
- other 7%
- Setúbal 16%
- Lisbon 68%

Brazilians
- other 14%
- Coimbra 3%
- Braga 3%
- Santarém 4%
- Aveiro 5%
- Faro 8%
- Setúbal 9%
- Porto 11%
- Lisbon 44%

Eastern Europeans
- Madeira 3%
- Coimbra 4%
- Braga 4%
- Aveiro 6%
- other 11%
- Lisbon 22%
- Setúbal 6%
- Leiria 7%
- Porto 9%
- Santarém 10%
- Faro 18%

Southern Europe was a major source of labour migrants for the industrial economies of northwest Europe during the early post-war decades. Since the 1980s, however, Greece, Italy, Portugal and Spain (and more recently Cyprus and Malta too) have become destinations for large numbers of immigrants, who have arrived from a great diversity of countries in Africa, South and East Asia, Latin America and, since 1990, Eastern Europe. Spain and Italy best exemplify this "super-diversity" of migrant origins; Portugal's immigrants have come mainly from Portuguese-speaking former colonies in Africa and from Brazil; Greece's from adjacent Albania and Bulgaria.

Several reasons account for this turnaround from mass emigration to mass immigration. Located on the southern flank of the EU, and with long coastlines facing migrant supply routes across the Mediterranean, these countries have been the first port of call for migrants coming from North and Sub-Saharan Africa and the Middle East. Greece's northern land border suddenly became porous after the fall of communism in its northern neighbours. The southern EU countries, in contrast to northern EU states, have developed a laissez-faire policy towards migrants, for whom entry has been relatively easy. They have entered on tourist visas and overstayed, or arrived clandestinely by boat, often on perilous voyages, and periodic amnesties have enabled erstwhile "illegal" migrants to regularize their status. But the most powerful explanatory factor has been the opportunities offered by the casual and informal labour markets of these countries, with plenty of jobs available in construction, tourism, agriculture, and domestic and care work – jobs which their own citizens no longer want to do.

Some of the new immigration flows are highly specific as regards nationality, gender and occupation. In Italy, for instance, most Filipinos are women working as domestic cleaners and carers in the cities, most

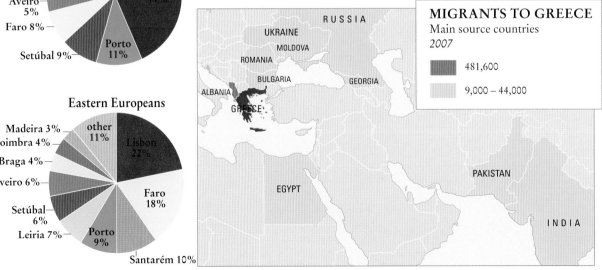

MIGRANTS TO GREECE
Main source countries
2007

- 481,600
- 9,000 – 44,000

RUSSIA, UKRAINE, MOLDOVA, ROMANIA, BULGARIA, GEORGIA, ALBANIA, GREECE, EGYPT, PAKISTAN, INDIA

Senegalese are men engaged in street-hawking in cities and tourist resorts, whilst Albanians and Romanians, despite their more recent arrival, are widely distributed both geographically and throughout various sectors of the labour market. In Portugal, immigrants from the Portuguese-speaking African countries are found overwhelmingly in Lisbon; Eastern Europeans are much more widely spread; whilst Brazilians have an intermediate level of concentration and dispersion, mostly in western districts. For all groups, regularization can be a first step towards family reunification, a more balanced age and sex distribution, and eventual permanent settlement.

MIGRANTS TO ITALY
Main source countries
2007

	400,000 – 625,300
	365,900
	100,000 – 157,000
	50,000 – 99,000

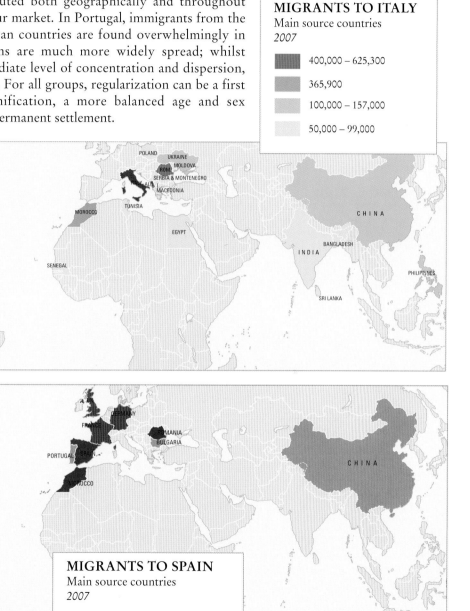

MIGRANTS TO SPAIN
Main source countries
2007

	400,000 – 706,200
	220,000 – 360,000
	100,000 – 163,000
	80,000 – 99,999

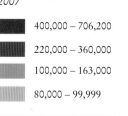

THE QUIET MIGRATION

In many high-income countries, family members of immigrants are eventually granted residence.

Migration to achieve family reunion has long been an important element of voluntary migration, featuring in European migration to the Americas and Australasia, and in Chinese migration to South-East Asia. But it became especially important after the first oil crisis of the early-mid 1970s.

At that time, racist and xenophobic electoral pressures on Western European political parties resulted in harsh restrictions being imposed on further primary migration of young-adult working-class males from Mediterranean countries and former colonial territories. This resulted in many split families, with male workers determined to hold on to their work and residence rights in Western Europe, while their family members remained in the countries of origin. In the context of the Cold War, Western European governments felt it necessary to demonstrate their humanitarianism by allowing close relatives, such as spouses/partners and non-adult offspring, to join their relatives. With other legal routes to settlement open only to those with professional qualifications or great wealth, family reunion has become the major form of immigration for many countries over much of the period since the 1970s.

70%
of immigration to USA involves family reunion

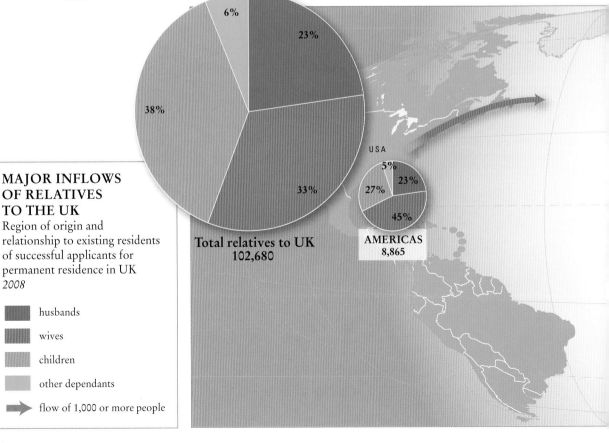

MAJOR INFLOWS OF RELATIVES TO THE UK
Region of origin and relationship to existing residents of successful applicants for permanent residence in UK
2008

- husbands
- wives
- children
- other dependants
- → flow of 1,000 or more people

Total relatives to UK
102,680

USA

AMERICAS
8,865

Family reunion accounts for about 60 percent of non-European immigration into the EU, and 70 percent of immigration into the USA. However, for a country such as Canada, which is still recruiting primary migrants, it represented only 27 percent of immigrants in 2001.

Critics from both xenophobic and progressive perspectives often argue that the family reunion route is being abused, pointing out that, through arranged or fraudulent marriages, many young men who are in effect labour migrants are able to by-pass immigration rules set up to exclude them. Efforts to stamp out abuse have sometimes led to excessive delays in the granting of permission to elderly parents, spouses and children attempting to join family members in high-income countries. Similar restrictions are placed on immigrants to the Gulf.

The policy to admit migrants for family reunification purposes is not universal. It is not normally allowed, for example, in East Asian countries, where immigrant non-nationals lacking qualifications or wealth are typically regarded (however long their residence in the country of destination) as temporary visitors rather than permanent settlers.

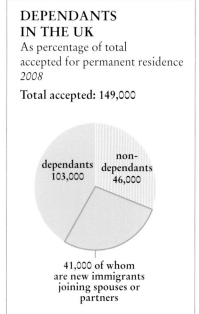

DEPENDANTS IN THE UK
As percentage of total accepted for permanent residence
2008

Total accepted: 149,000

dependants 103,000

non-dependants 46,000

41,000 of whom are new immigrants joining spouses or partners

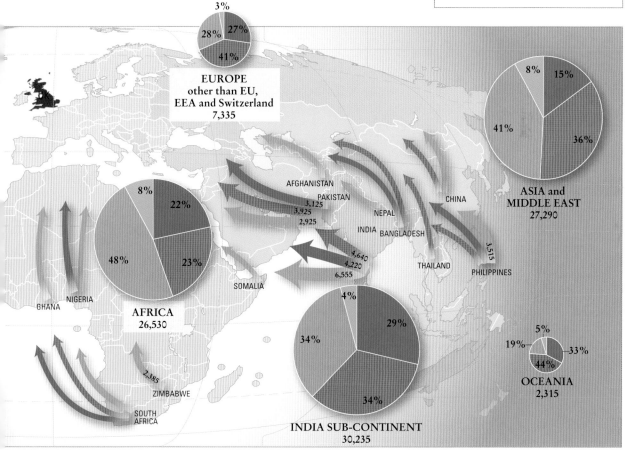

3%
27%
28%
41%

EUROPE
other than EU, EEA and Switzerland
7,335

8%
15%
41%
36%

ASIA and MIDDLE EAST
27,290

AFGHANISTAN 3,125
PAKISTAN 3,925
NEPAL 2,925
CHINA
INDIA
BANGLADESH
THAILAND
PHILIPPINES 3,515

8%
22%
48%
23%

AFRICA
26,530

GHANA
NIGERIA
SOMALIA

4,640
4,220
6,555

ZIMBABWE
2,385

SOUTH AFRICA

4%
29%
34%
34%

INDIA SUB-CONTINENT
30,235

5%
19%
44%
33%

OCEANIA
2,315

47

LATIN AMERICA

During the 20th century, Latin America shifted from being a subcontinent of immigration to one of emigration.

Since the arrival of the first Europeans in the late 15th century, the Americas have been one of the great destinations of migration. Today, only the USA and Canada retain that position. Latin America has shifted from being a subcontinent of immigration to one of emigration in an almost mirror image to that of the migration transitions in Southern Europe and parts of East Asia. This reverse transition has, nevertheless, been accompanied by intense urbanization as well as by relatively small but significant flows into the interior.

The net emigration for Central America is almost 12 million people, a figure mainly explained by the huge movement from Mexico to the USA. A further net outflow of 3.3 million has occurred from South America, again dominated by migration to the north. However, the migration from South America has been less unidirectional than that from Central America and Mexico. Significant flows have taken place to Europe – in particular to Spain – echoing old colonial and language ties. Another significant "return flow" has been to Japan from Brazil and Peru. Since 1990, descendants of Japanese settlers from the 1920s and 1930s have been recruited into factory employment in Japan.

Latin America is one of the most highly urbanized parts of the world. With 77 percent of its population classified as urban in mid-2007, the region is dominated by international migration from and to the largest cities. Migration within South America has been primarily between neighbouring states, with Argentina the largest regional destination. Mexico is a major transit route to the USA from elsewhere in Central America, and is host to large numbers of Guatemalans, for example. Mexico has also received a significant number of migrants from the USA, as Mexicans return home with their US-born children.

The Hispanic population within the USA has grown both in number and in terms of the proportion it represents of the total population. Although it is found throughout the whole of the USA, it is concentrated in the southern and western states, and in Texas, New Mexico, and Southern California, in particular.

15 million more people left than arrived in Latin America 1950–2000

GROWING NUMBER OF HISPANICS IN THE USA
Number of people and proportion of population in USA identifying themselves as Hispanics or Spanish-speaking
1970–2005

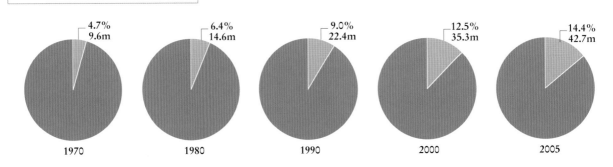

1970	1980	1990	2000	2005
4.7% 9.6m	6.4% 14.6m	9.0% 22.4m	12.5% 35.3m	14.4% 42.7m

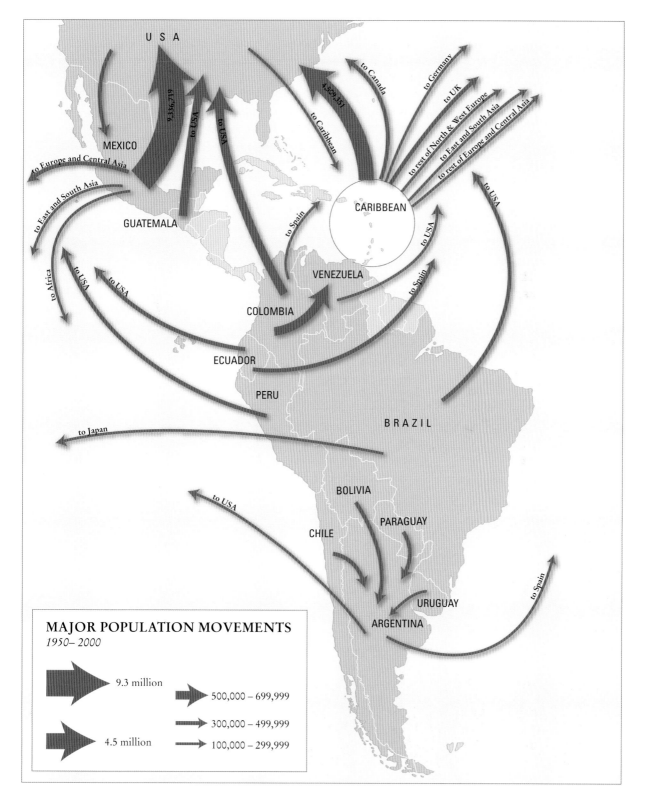

USA

to Canada

to Germany

to UK

to rest of North & West Europe

to East and South Asia

to rest of Europe and Central Asia

9,336,719

to USA

to USA

4,509,351

to Caribbean

MEXICO

to Europe and Central Asia

to East and South Asia

GUATEMALA

to Africa

to USA

to USA

CARIBBEAN

to USA

to USA

to Spain

VENEZUELA

to Spain

COLOMBIA

ECUADOR

PERU

to USA

BRAZIL

to Japan

BOLIVIA

PARAGUAY

CHILE

to USA

URUGUAY

to Spain

ARGENTINA

MAJOR POPULATION MOVEMENTS
1950– 2000

9.3 million

500,000 – 699,999

4.5 million

300,000 – 499,999

100,000 – 299,999

THE GULF

Rapid economic expansion, fuelled by oil wealth, has created millions of jobs, most filled by migrant workers.

Bahrain, Kuwait, Oman, Qatar, Saudi Arabia, and the United Arab Emirates (UAE) together form the Gulf Cooperation Council (GCC). Foreign nationals make up a higher proportion of the populations of countries in this region than anywhere else in the world, more than 50 percent on average. Jordan, which is not a GCC member, is the only other country to have a comparable proportion of its population made up of foreign nationals, but it hosts a very large number of refugees, first Palestinian, and, more recently, Iraqi, whereas the GCC countries have virtually no refugees. Their immigrant population consists exclusively of labour migrants.

Demand for labour was associated initially with the discovery of oil, which occurred as recently as 1966 in Dubai, in the UAE. The population of the UAE was only 180,000 at the time, including a few thousand foreign nationals, but by 2010 it had an estimated population of 4.4 million, including 3.3 million foreign nationals. The tremendous growth of the immigrant population helped the continued economic rise of the region.

This economic expansion was initially fuelled by oil wealth; most jobs were associated with the oil industry, and in construction. Some effort has been made to diversify economies away from oil, most spectacularly in Dubai, and labour has been required in other sectors, such as tourism. There is also an increased demand for skilled professionals in management, medicine, law, and education, which is also being met largely by migrant workers.

These workers come from all over the world, although South Asia, and in particular India, accounts for the largest number. There are an estimated 2.2 million Indians in the UAE, and 1.3 million in Saudi Arabia, making India–UAE and India–Saudi Arabia the fourth and ninth most significant migration corridors in the world in 2010, in terms of absolute numbers.

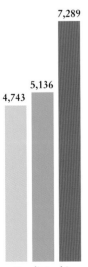

A RAPIDLY INCREASING MIGRANT WORKFORCE

Number of migrant workers
in country
1990–2010
thousands

- 1990
- 2000
- 2010

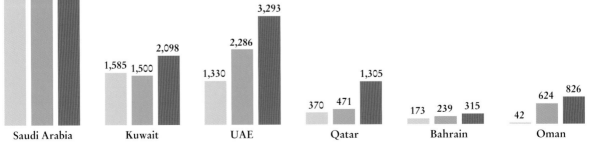

Saudi Arabia: 4,743 / 5,136 / 7,289
Kuwait: 1,585 / 1,500 / 2,098
UAE: 1,330 / 2,286 / 3,293
Qatar: 370 / 471 / 1,305
Bahrain: 173 / 239 / 315
Oman: 42 / 624 / 826

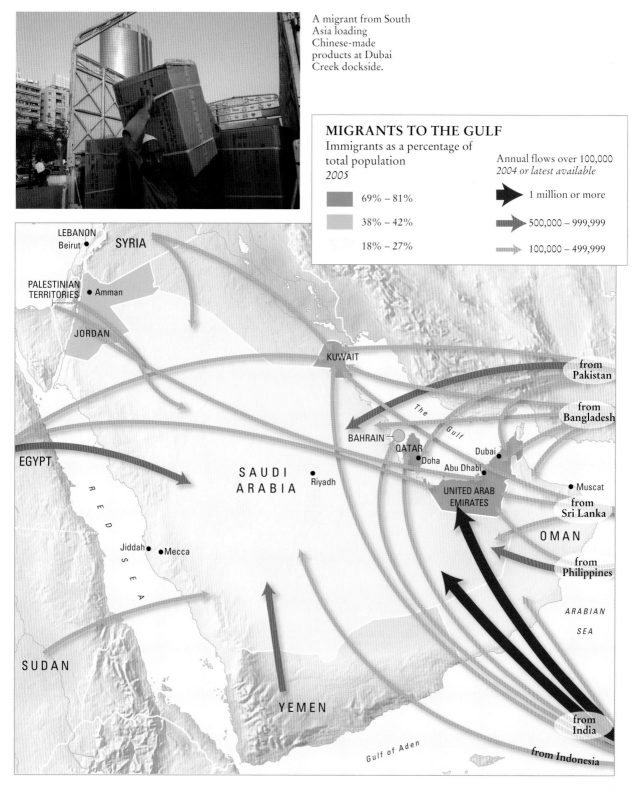

A migrant from South Asia loading Chinese-made products at Dubai Creek dockside.

MIGRANTS TO THE GULF

Immigrants as a percentage of total population
2005

- 69% – 81%
- 38% – 42%
- 18% – 27%

Annual flows over 100,000
2004 or latest available

- 1 million or more
- 500,000 – 999,999
- 100,000 – 499,999

LEBANON
Beirut
SYRIA

PALESTINIAN TERRITORIES
Amman
JORDAN

KUWAIT

from Pakistan

from Bangladesh

EGYPT

BAHRAIN
QATAR
Doha
Abu Dhabi
Dubai
UNITED ARAB EMIRATES

The Gulf

SAUDI ARABIA
Riyadh

Muscat

from Sri Lanka

OMAN

from Philippines

RED SEA

Jiddah
Mecca

ARABIAN SEA

SUDAN

YEMEN

from India

Gulf of Aden

from Indonesia

MIGRATION PATTERNS IN EURASIA

A new Eurasian migration system is bringing migrant workers to Russia's booming oil, gas and industrial centres.

The fall of the Iron Curtain in 1989, followed by the collapse of the Soviet Union in 1991, resulted in three major changes in migration patterns. First, migration flows from Central and Eastern European countries became focused westwards towards the countries of the EU – a process facilitated by German reunification in 1990, and by the EU enlargements of 2004 and 2007. Secondly, a mass migration occurred of peoples who now suddenly found themselves members of ethnic minorities in the successor states of the Soviet Union (for example, Russians in Ukraine, Kazakhstan and the Baltic states). About 25 million ethnic Russians lived in the successor states in 1991; of these about 11 million migrated (many under pressure) to Russia in the following 10 years, with about 4 million non-Russians moving in the opposite direction.

Thirdly, a new Eurasian migration system has emerged. This focuses on Moscow, St. Petersburg, and on other centres of industrial development, including oil and gas production. Migrants come from Russia's own distant provinces, such as the Russian Far East and Eastern Siberia, from its new

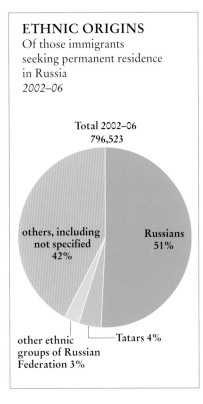

ETHNIC ORIGINS
Of those immigrants seeking permanent residence in Russia
2002–06

Total 2002–06
796,523

- others, including not specified 42%
- Russians 51%
- Tatars 4%
- other ethnic groups of Russian Federation 3%

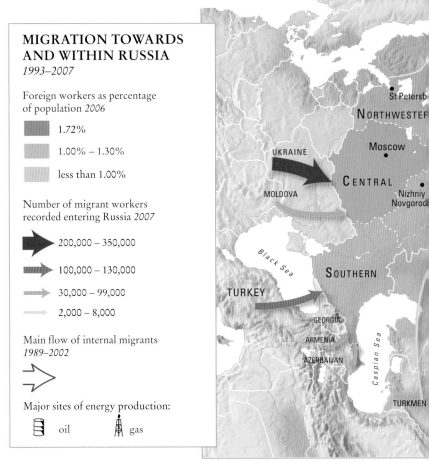

MIGRATION TOWARDS AND WITHIN RUSSIA
1993–2007

Foreign workers as percentage of population *2006*
- 1.72%
- 1.00% – 1.30%
- less than 1.00%

Number of migrant workers recorded entering Russia *2007*
- 200,000 – 350,000
- 100,000 – 130,000
- 30,000 – 99,000
- 2,000 – 8,000

Main flow of internal migrants *1989–2002*

Major sites of energy production:
- oil
- gas

"near abroad" countries – the successor states in Central Asia and the Caucasus that still enjoy visa-free entry – and from "far abroad" countries such as China, Turkey, and Vietnam. Around 40 percent of foreign migrants work in the construction industry.

The registered immigrant foreign worker population in Russia in 2007 was over 2 million, with maybe another 6 million living and working in the country without permission. As is often the case, most of the foreign workers do the jobs that locals avoid, but complex intersections of class and ethnicity can result. In many Siberian and Far Eastern cities, for example, ethnic Russians do all the white-collar jobs, and act as the owners/managers on building sites and in factories. Manual workers are often Chinese, and Chinese traders also have a strong presence in the local markets (often entering on tourist visas). However, the unemployed underclass – those engaged in petty criminal activity, and drug and alcohol abuse – are often ethnic Russians.

More than **10%** *of the population of six districts in the Russian Far East emigrated 1993–2002*

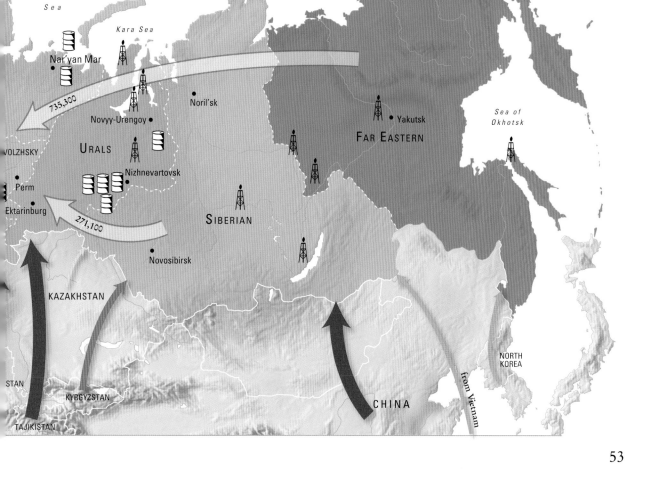

MIGRATION WITHIN INDIA

Around a quarter of people in India have changed their place of residence at least once in their lifetime.

The 2001 census showed that 268 million Indians had moved within the country at some time in their life. The vast majority had moved only short distances, often for marriage, but over 41 million had moved to a different state, with one quarter of these having moved during the five years before the census. By contrast, the number of Indians and people of Indian descent estimated to be outside India amounted to only about 18.5 million. As in most countries of the world, the number of internal migrants far exceeds the number of international migrants.

The largest flows of migrants are to the states in which the country's largest cities – Mumbai and Delhi – are located, and also to other more developed states such as Punjab. Patterns have changed over time, however. For example, migration to Kolkata and other parts of West Bengal has steadily diminished since the 1970s. By 2001, West Bengal was no longer one of the more dynamic states as regards economic growth. Two of the poorest states, Bihar and Uttar Pradesh, continue to be significant origins of migration.

The ten-year migration that took place between the 1991 and 2001 censuses shows a marked increase in the total volume of internal migration, which has also become more oriented towards urban areas. In 1971, for example, rural-to-urban migration accounted for just over one in four internal migrants during the previous ten years, while in 2001, that proportion had increased to almost two in five.

The movement from rural to urban areas was dominated by men. In 2001, almost 150 men moved from rural to urban areas for every 100 women. In the movement of people between rural areas, however, women equal or outnumber men, suggesting that this movement is dominated by women moving away from home for marriage. Within urban areas, the flow was more balanced, with a migration of families as well as single men and women.

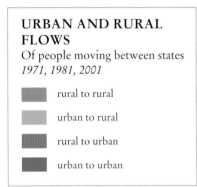

URBAN AND RURAL FLOWS
Of people moving between states
1971, 1981, 2001

- rural to rural
- urban to rural
- rural to urban
- urban to urban

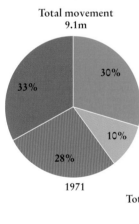

Total movement
9.1m

30%
10%
28%
33%

1971

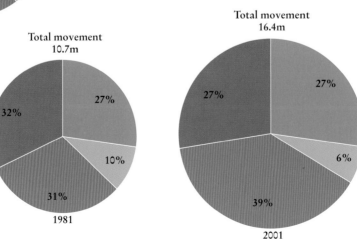

Total movement
10.7m

27%
10%
31%
32%

1981

Total movement
16.4m

27%
6%
39%
27%

2001

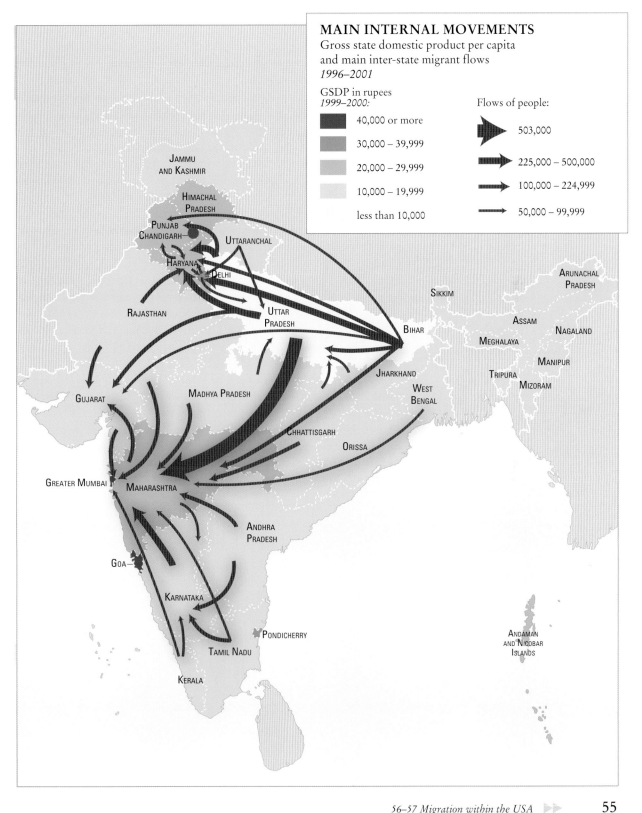

MAIN INTERNAL MOVEMENTS
Gross state domestic product per capita
and main inter-state migrant flows
1996–2001

GSDP in rupees
1999–2000:

40,000 or more

30,000 – 39,999

20,000 – 29,999

10,000 – 19,999

less than 10,000

Flows of people:

503,000

225,000 – 500,000

100,000 – 224,999

50,000 – 99,999

JAMMU
AND KASHMIR

HIMACHAL
PRADESH

PUNJAB
CHANDIGARH

UTTARANCHAL

HARYANA

DELHI

RAJASTHAN

UTTAR
PRADESH

SIKKIM

ARUNACHAL
PRADESH

ASSAM

NAGALAND

MEGHALAYA

MANIPUR

TRIPURA

MIZORAM

BIHAR

JHARKHAND

WEST
BENGAL

GUJARAT

MADHYA PRADESH

CHHATTISGARH

ORISSA

GREATER MUMBAI

MAHARASHTRA

ANDHRA
PRADESH

GOA

KARNATAKA

PONDICHERRY

ANDAMAN
AND NICOBAR
ISLANDS

TAMIL NADU

KERALA

MIGRATION WITHIN THE USA

Migration within the USA occurs for a range of reasons, many based on personal preference.

The USA is an unusually mobile, politically stable, and uniquely wealthy country, and the patterns of population movement within it provide a fine example of migration decisions made on the basis of choice rather than from necessity.

Surveys of the reasons why people migrate within the USA indicate that housing and neighbourhood factors predominately influence local moves, but for migrations over longer distances within the country, job and career development, and family considerations come to the fore, with study, retirement, health and climate factors also significant. For immigrants to the USA, employment factors massively dominate all others, although family and study are also given as reasons.

In conjunction with broader economic trends such as the decline of the "rustbelt" cities of northern and northeastern USA, and the growth of the "sunbelt" cities of the south, the effects of these reasons for migrating can be seen in the net migration rates for the period from 2001 to 2008. These indicate a strong tendency for people to leave the most urbanized states in favour of the less urbanized, with high net losses from New York, District of Columbia, New Jersey and Michigan. There is also a shift from north to south, and a move towards environmentally attractive states such as Florida and Arizona.

At the metropolitan level, the major gainers from internal migration are regional cities, often those with recreational activities (Phoenix, Atlanta, Las Vegas), while the major losers are the "global" cities of New York, Los Angeles and Chicago. Cities such as Miami and San Francisco, which were most likely to gain in the past, have become net losers through outward internal migration. Inward-bound international migrants have, to a certain extent, filled the gaps left by the domestic migrants in California, Illinois and New York.

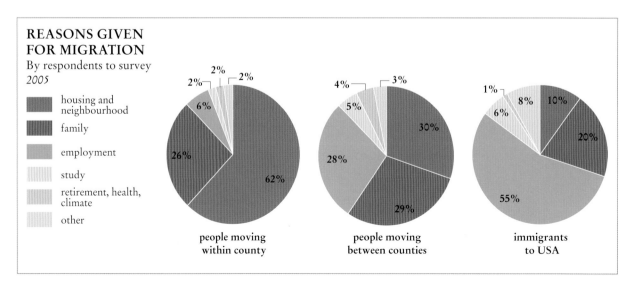

REASONS GIVEN FOR MIGRATION
By respondents to survey *2005*

- housing and neighbourhood
- family
- employment
- study
- retirement, health, climate
- other

people moving within county
62%, 26%, 6%, 2%, 2%, 2%

people moving between counties
30%, 29%, 28%, 5%, 4%, 3%

immigrants to USA
55%, 20%, 10%, 8%, 6%, 1%

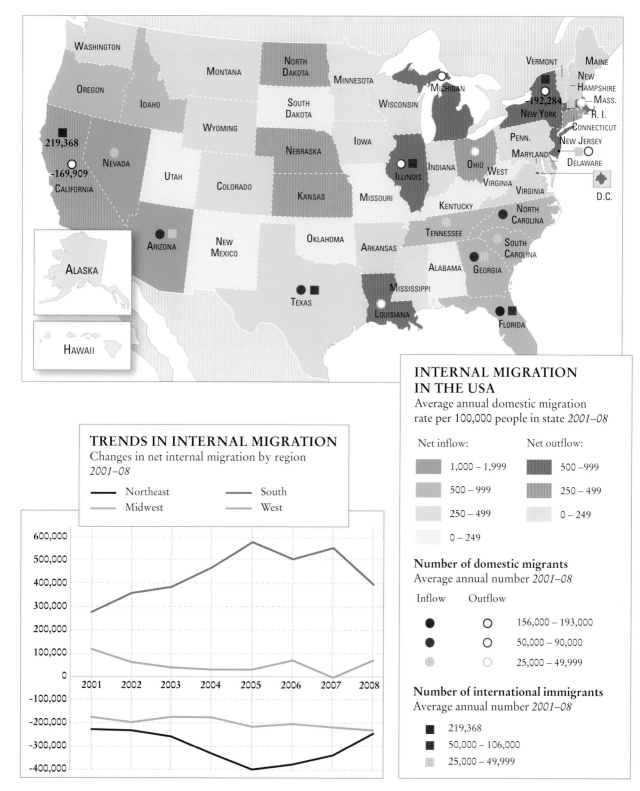

INTERNAL MIGRATION IN THE USA
Average annual domestic migration rate per 100,000 people in state *2001–08*

Net inflow:
- 1,000 – 1,999
- 500 – 999
- 250 – 499
- 0 – 249

Net outflow:
- 500 –999
- 250 – 499
- 0 – 249

Number of domestic migrants
Average annual number *2001–08*

Inflow / Outflow
- 156,000 – 193,000
- 50,000 – 90,000
- 25,000 – 49,999

Number of international immigrants
Average annual number *2001–08*
- 219,368
- 50,000 – 106,000
- 25,000 – 49,999

TRENDS IN INTERNAL MIGRATION
Changes in net internal migration by region *2001–08*

- Northeast
- Midwest
- South
- West

57

INTERNAL MIGRATION & POVERTY

Poor people are more likely to migrate for work within their own country than abroad.

Discussions about the relationship between migration and development often assume that the primary issue of concern is international migration from poor to rich nations. Yet, in practice, most poor people move over relatively short distances, for relatively short periods of time. This is generally easier to organize and cheaper than overseas migration, and usually allows migrants to maintain strong links with their families.

There were around 65 million rural workers living outside their province of origin in China in 2006, the overwhelming majority working in manufacturing and service industries. This represents around a quarter of the rural workforce, and is a migration dominated by men in their twenties. Most likely to leave are those with junior secondary education. The very poor and uneducated are unlikely to move at all. The predominant movement is towards the rapidly industrializing east, although the global economic downturn since 2008 may provoke a reversal of these flows. The factories of Guangdong attract the largest number of migrants; there is also a much smaller, but no less significant, flow of white-collar workers heading for professional, technical and managerial jobs in Beijing and Shanghai.

It is not just huge countries that have large numbers of internal migrants. In much of the Savannah belt of West Africa, migration to Europe is only a dream for people from poor families, whereas almost anyone can move internally, so long as they can afford the bus fare. In Ghana, as much as half of the population can be considered "migrants", in the sense of having spent at least a year living outside their district of birth. Over the five years preceding the last census in 2000, there was a net flow away from the northern and eastern regions of the country towards the centre and south, and especially to the major cities of Accra and Kumasi. These internal migrants were, on average, better educated than those who had not moved at all.

INTERNAL MIGRATION IN GHANA

Major flows between provinces
1995–2000

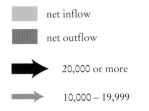

net inflow

net outflow

20,000 or more

10,000 – 19,999

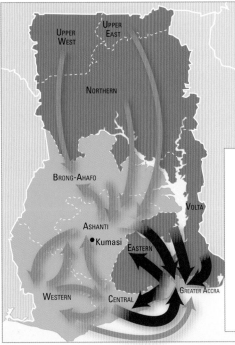

LEVEL OF EDUCATION

Maximum level of education completed by migrant workers compared with that of general population
2000

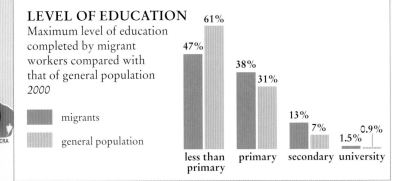

migrants

general population

	less than primary	primary	secondary	university
migrants	47%	38%	13%	1.5%
general population	61%	31%	7%	0.9%

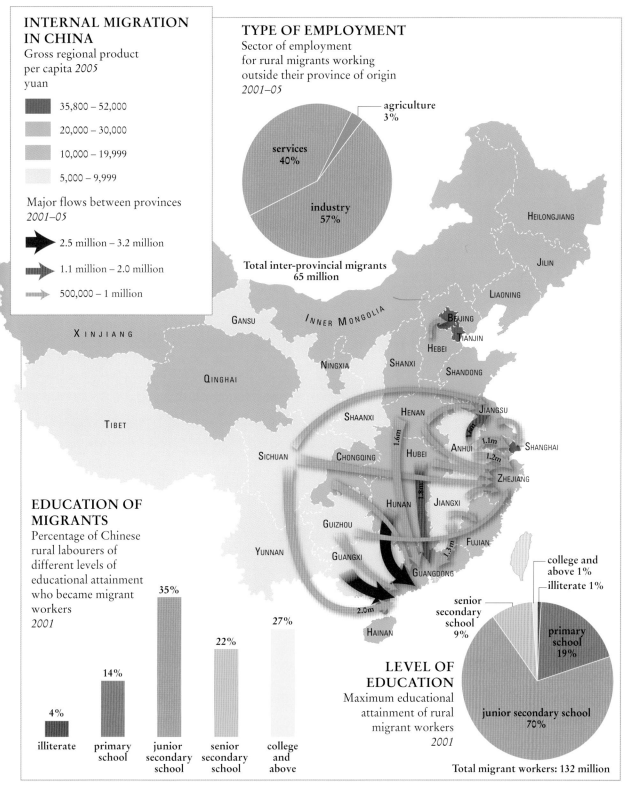

INTERNAL MIGRATION IN CHINA

Gross regional product
per capita 2005
yuan

- 35,800 – 52,000
- 20,000 – 30,000
- 10,000 – 19,999
- 5,000 – 9,999

Major flows between provinces
2001–05

- 2.5 million – 3.2 million
- 1.1 million – 2.0 million
- 500,000 – 1 million

TYPE OF EMPLOYMENT

Sector of employment
for rural migrants working
outside their province of origin
2001–05

agriculture
3%

services
40%

industry
57%

Total inter-provincial migrants
65 million

EDUCATION OF MIGRANTS

Percentage of Chinese
rural labourers of
different levels of
educational attainment
who became migrant
workers
2001

- illiterate 4%
- primary school 14%
- junior secondary school 35%
- senior secondary school 22%
- college and above 27%

LEVEL OF EDUCATION

Maximum educational
attainment of rural
migrant workers
2001

college and above 1%
illiterate 1%
primary school 19%
senior secondary school 9%
junior secondary school 70%

Total migrant workers: 132 million

HEILONGJIANG
JILIN
LIAONING
BEIJING
TIANJIN
HEBEI
GANSU
INNER MONGOLIA
XINJIANG
QINGHAI
NINGXIA
SHANXI
SHANDONG
TIBET
SHAANXI
HENAN
JIANGSU
SICHUAN
CHONGQING
HUBEI
ANHUI
SHANGHAI
ZHEJIANG
HUNAN
JIANGXI
GUIZHOU
FUJIAN
YUNNAN
GUANGXI
GUANGDONG
HAINAN

1.6m
1.6m
1.1m
1.2m
1.3m
1.3m
2.0m

Part Three

THE AGE OF MIGRATION: HYBRID IDENTITIES OF HUMAN MOBILITY

Over the past 20 or so years human mobility has accelerated and diversified, and also become increasingly globalized and politicized. In contrast to the characteristic migrations of the past – transatlantic settler migration, or post-war "guest-worker" migration – today's migrants are more socially and demographically varied, and exhibit an increasing heterogeneity of forms of mobility and reasons for moving.

The maps in this part of the atlas explore key topics of this diverse mosaic of current human mobility. The first six look at refugees, asylum seekers and displaced persons. Although the number of recognized refugees is only about 5 percent of all international migrants, the total number of "persons of concern" is two or three times greater. Equally significant, in numerical and humanitarian terms, are the internally displaced, expelled from their homes by violent conflict, environmental disasters (flood, earthquake, volcanic eruption), or dam construction. For the future, "climate refugees" are both a contested concept and subject to wide-ranging numerical speculation.

If refugees and displaced persons reflect a history of risk, so too does irregular migration, which is particularly intense across border areas separating poor from rich countries, such as the Mexico-US frontier, or the Mediterranean Sea. Increasing securitization of borders forces migrants to take greater risks, and some pay the ultimate price.

The age of migration increasingly sees new flows defined by the social, educational and demographic characteristics of the migrants. Gender is a crucial variable underlying migration patterns: the "feminization" of migration reflects the globalization of domestic and care work, as well as the increasing number of women (fewer men) who migrate for marriage. Age, education and social class frame the maps on child, student, skilled, and retirement migration.

Earlier waves and generations of migrants face other options. Some return, sooner or later, to their country of origin. Those who stay on face the issue of the extent to which they feel motivated, or are encouraged, to "integrate" in their host societies, and how much they want to stay in touch with their home countries, for instance by voting or sending remittances. This is not a zero-sum game. Successful integration can go hand-in-hand with the maintenance of strong transnational links to origin countries, and hybrid identities, and back-and-forth mobilities, can result, often institutionalized via dual nationality.

Some of the Zimbabweans who made an illegal border crossing into South Africa at the time of the disputed presidential election in 2008.

61

Refugees

People who have fled their country through fear of persecution are refugees in international law, but some states are reluctant to grant them this status.

The UN Convention relating to the Status of Refugees (1951), which gives refugees their official status, dates from the aftermath of the Second World War, when millions of people in Europe found themselves stateless. Until the mid-1990s, the global number of refugees grew substantially, as anti-colonial wars in Africa, and proxy wars between the USA and the Soviet Union gave way to wars with more diverse causes, such as the complex emergencies in the Balkans and Rwanda in the 1990s. Since then, the official number of refugees has fallen slightly. Although this partly reflects the resolution of some major conflicts, it is also a function of the increasing reluctance of states to recognize refugees. Indeed, the rise in numbers since 2005 is because people in refugee-like situations who have not been officially classified as refugees are now included in the figures.

Measures to contain conflict and displacement within national boundaries have led to a large rise in the number of people classified as "internally displaced", and there has also been an increase in the officially "stateless", adding to the total number of persons of concern

> The term **refugee** shall apply to any person who, owing to well-founded fear of being persecuted for reasons of race, religion, nationality, membership of a particular social group or political opinion, is outside the country of his nationality and is unable, or owing to such fear, is unwilling to avail himself of the protection of that country.
>
> *UN Convention relating to the Status of Refugees, 1951, Article 1*

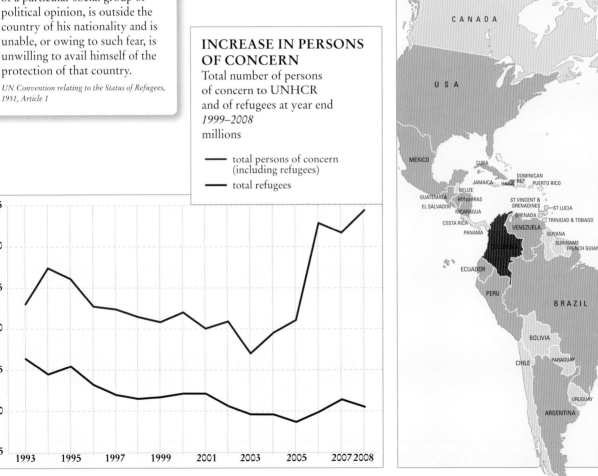

INCREASE IN PERSONS OF CONCERN
Total number of persons of concern to UNHCR and of refugees at year end
1999–2008
millions

— total persons of concern (including refugees)
— total refugees

to the United Nations High Commissioner for Refugees (UNHCR).

The refugee problem is a global issue, with the main countries of origin and destination being among the poorest. Since the 1980s, Afghanistan has been the largest producer of refugees, and Africa the most severely affected continent. While those in the industrialized countries assume that most refugees try to move to Europe or North America, this is far from true. Pakistan and Iran have long received the most refugees.

It is often assumed that hosting refugees represents a significant burden for receiving countries. Yet, the consequences are much more varied. For example, high-profile refugees in the past famously include Nobel Prize-winning physicist Albert Einstein, and many other refugees – skilled and unskilled – have made substantial contributions in their adopted countries. And while the UNHCR is the main international body responsible for refugees, assistance is provided to refugees by a wide range of governments, NGOs, and ordinary people.

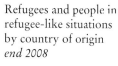
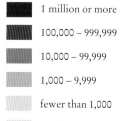

REFUGEES
Refugees and people in refugee-like situations by country of origin
end 2008

1 million or more
100,000 – 999,999
10,000 – 99,999
1,000 – 9,999
fewer than 1,000
no data

Receiving countries
Number of refugees per 1,000 population

40 – 80
10 – 30

REFUGEE WAREHOUSING

The majority of the world's refugees have waited more than five years for a solution to their exile.

efugee camps provide a political rather than a humanitarian solution to refugee displacement. They offer a way of restricting refugees' movement and ensuring that their welfare is not the responsibility of the host government but is undertaken by the international community, usually through the United Nations High Commissioner for Refugees (UNHCR). Palestinian refugees in the Middle East have, since 1949, been the responsibility of the United Nations Relief and Works Agency (UNRWA)

Refugees living in camps are often vulnerable to serious human rights violations. Their movement is limited, and living conditions are cramped, creating a situation in which physical and sexual abuse is common. As exile extends to years, lives are wasted and entire generations are denied the skills that would help them rebuild their society.

During the violence of the immediate post-Cold War period, the refugee population increased, and people spent longer and longer in

WAREHOUSED REFUGEES

Location and number of refugees under care of UNHCR in Africa, Balkans, Middle East and West Asia
2004

- 1 million – 2 million
- 400,000 – 830,000
- 100,000 – 240,000
- 25,000 – 99,999
- refugees registered with UNRWA

Symbol colour indicates refugee country of origin

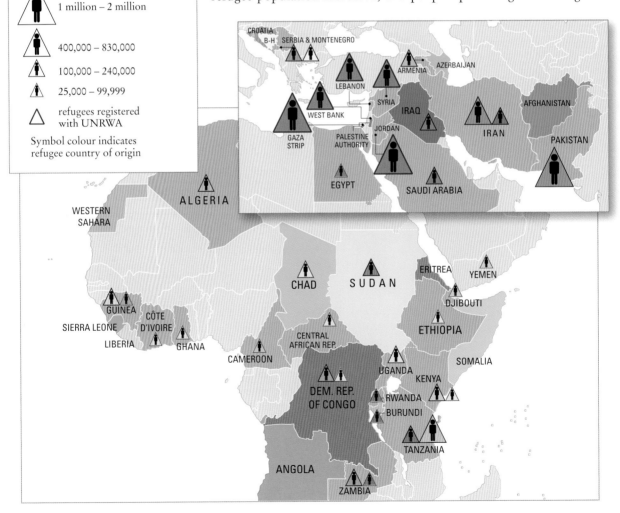

camps, as countries were reluctant to offer shelter. In 2004, the US Committee on Refugees and Immigrants initiated an "anti-warehousing" campaign to draw attention to this abuse of rights, and a resolution to the situation became a more urgent priority. The UNHCR Standing Committee defined a "protracted refugee situation" as more than 25,000 people who had been waiting for a permanent solution to their displacement for more than five years.

UNHCR considers three possible "durable solutions" for refugees: return to their country of origin, integration in the country where they are living, and resettlement to a third country. Substantial return of refugees usually depends on the end of conflict, but the second and third solutions are possible even if conflicts continue. More substantial efforts to generate the political will for integration or resettlement have been in evidence since 2004. In December 2008, the annual High Commissioners Dialogue was devoted to the issue, and UNHCR is promoting the use of regional Comprehensive Plans of Action to find solutions in which all actors may be involved.

Around 14,000 Karen refugees from Burma live in this camp in Thailand. Many have been housed in similar camps for 30 years.

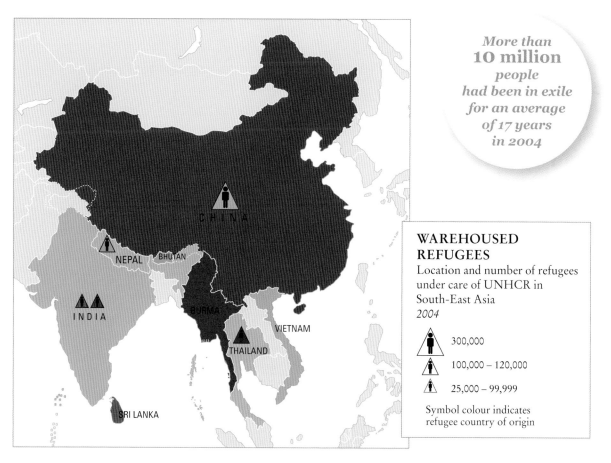

More than
10 million
*people
had been in exile
for an average
of 17 years
in 2004*

WAREHOUSED REFUGEES
Location and number of refugees under care of UNHCR in South-East Asia
2004

300,000

100,000 – 120,000

25,000 – 99,999

Symbol colour indicates refugee country of origin

REFUGEE RETURN

A sizable number of refugees have returned to their countries of origin since the mid-1990s.

Despite international attention to flows of asylum-seekers and refugees, a surprisingly large number of refugees have returned to their country of origin since the mid-1990s. High-profile returns following the end of armed conflict and/or "regime change" have taken place in countries such as Rwanda (1996), states in the former Yugoslavia (1996–99) and Afghanistan (since 2002), facilitated by organizations such as the UNHCR and the International Organization for Migration (IOM). In addition, refugees from a number of other conflict-affected countries have also sought to return to their home countries for a variety of economic, family and other reasons, often outside the context of official policy.

Many of the factors affecting the decision of refugees to return are the same as those that motivate migration and return more generally – economic conditions, or perceptions of political stability, bearing in mind that the judgments of individual refugees may be different from those of governments and international organizations. But in some contexts – notably Bosnia, Kosovo and Sri Lanka – there has been significant investment in information systems designed to provide potential returnees with reliable and up-to-date information about the

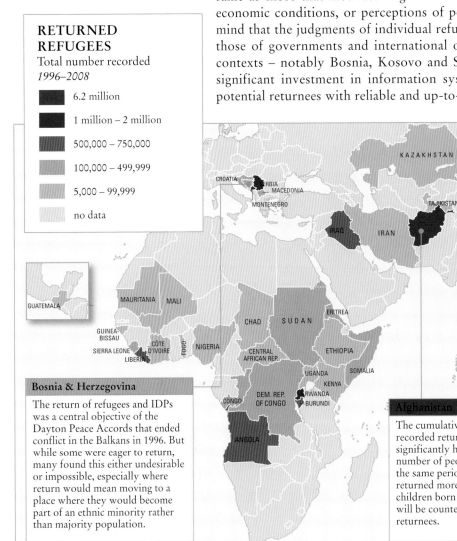

RETURNED REFUGEES

Total number recorded
1996–2008

- 6.2 million
- 1 million – 2 million
- 500,000 – 750,000
- 100,000 – 499,999
- 5,000 – 99,999
- no data

Bosnia & Herzegovina

The return of refugees and IDPs was a central objective of the Dayton Peace Accords that ended conflict in the Balkans in 1996. But while some were eager to return, many found this either undesirable or impossible, especially where return would mean moving to a place where they would become part of an ethnic minority rather than majority population.

Afghanistan

The cumulative total of 5 million recorded returning refugees is significantly higher than the total number of people displaced over the same period. People may have returned more than once, and children born outside the country will be counted amongst the returnees.

conditions for return. Social, cultural and family-related factors are also likely to be important. Refugees may decide to return as a result of the death or illness of a family member, even if this involves political or economic risks and might not "objectively" be a rational decision.

It is not easy accurately to gauge the number of returnees, and the aggregated figure may end up larger than the estimated number who fled. This may be because the same individual has returned more than once, or because returning families often include children who were born outside a country or area.

A key concern is whether the return of refugees is sustainable or not. International organizations are understandably nervous of promoting return if there is a risk that people will be unable to find employment, get caught up in political violence, or exacerbate conflicts – and be forced to flee again. However, there are also sometimes overpowering political incentives to promote return that may override such concerns.

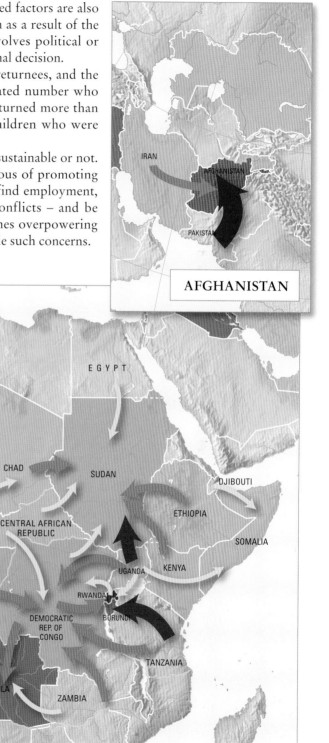

AFRICA

AFGHANISTAN

FLOWS OF RETURNEES
Number recorded as returning
2007–08

640,000

123,000 – 134,500

10,000 – 45,000

1,000 – 7,500

SEEKING ASYLUM IN EUROPE

The pattern of asylum seeking is closely related to patterns of conflict and human rights abuses.

While people seeking asylum in a country may be considered by its citizens as a single group, they come from a wide range of countries that change over time, depending on patterns of conflict or human rights abuse. Even people from a single country will be differentiated by ethnicity, age, gender, sexuality, and political or religious affiliation, all of which may be factors contributing to the persecution they faced in their country of origin.

Despite the focus on asylum seekers in the industrialized world, wealthier countries have a much smaller share of people claiming asylum than do poorer ones. They also have the resources to determine each claim individually. In European Union (EU) countries, officials decide if a claim matches the criteria set out in the 1951 UN Convention relating to the Status of Refugees. If it does, the asylum seeker is supported as a refugee; if it does not, a lower standard of temporary protection may be offered, or the claimant may be required to leave the country, in which case they are barred from claiming asylum in any other EU country.

There have been attempts to harmonize the asylum decision-making process between EU member states since the mid-1980s, although the development of supranational policy did not begin until 1999, when EU institutions were able to initiate legislation. More than ten major pieces of asylum legislation now govern everything from reception conditions for refugees to the ways in which failed asylum seekers can be removed. Nevertheless, despite this, asylum systems remain firmly in the hands of national governments, and the ways asylum regulations are applied across Europe can lead to very different recognition rates.

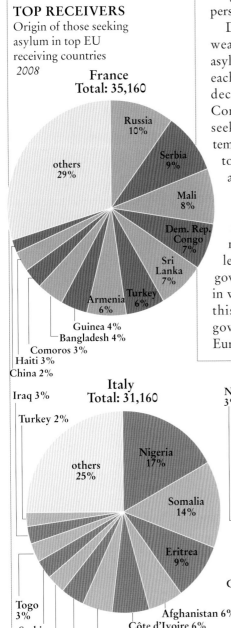

TOP RECEIVERS

Origin of those seeking asylum in top EU receiving countries
2008

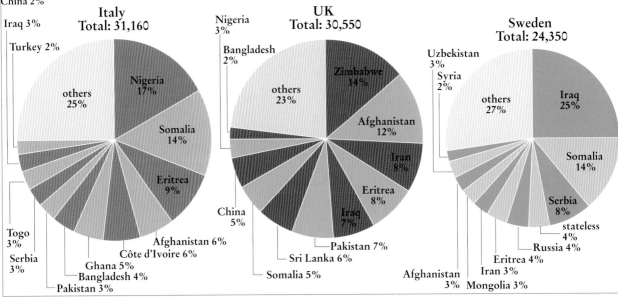

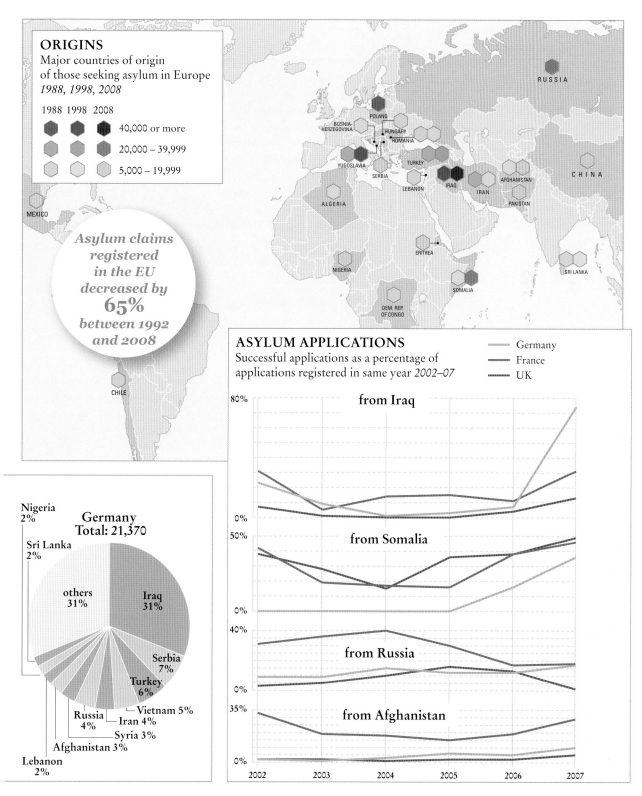

ORIGINS

Major countries of origin
of those seeking asylum in Europe
1988, 1998, 2008

1988 1998 2008

40,000 or more

20,000 – 39,999

5,000 – 19,999

Asylum claims registered in the EU decreased by **65%** *between 1992 and 2008*

RUSSIA

BOSNIA-HERZEGOVINA
POLAND
HUNGARY
ROMANIA
YUGOSLAVIA
SERBIA
TURKEY
LEBANON
IRAQ
IRAN
AFGHANISTAN
PAKISTAN
ALGERIA
CHINA
MEXICO
ERITREA
NIGERIA
SRI LANKA
SOMALIA
DEM. REP. OF CONGO
CHILE

ASYLUM APPLICATIONS

Successful applications as a percentage of
applications registered in same year *2002–07*

— Germany
— France
— UK

from Iraq

80%

0%

50%

from Somalia

0%

40%

from Russia

0%

35%

from Afghanistan

0%

2002   2003   2004   2005   2006   2007

Germany
Total: 21,370

Nigeria 2%

Sri Lanka 2%

others 31%

Iraq 31%

Serbia 7%

Turkey 6%

Vietnam 5%

Iran 4%

Russia 4%

Syria 3%

Afghanistan 3%

Lebanon 2%

INTERNALLY DISPLACED PERSONS

There are more IDPs than refugees, yet there are no official mechanisms for the international community to protect them.

There are an estimated 26 million Internally Displaced Persons (IDPs) – people who have been forced to leave their homes because of conflict, yet remain within their own country. This is a consequence of two trends: an increase in the number of conflicts within countries, and a decrease in the willingness of states to assist foreign nationals fleeing from such conflicts. In some cases, IDPs may be actively prevented from crossing an international border by state or quasi-state agents; in other cases IDPs may prefer to remain close to home, in the hope of returning quickly when conflict has ended, or in order to maintain contacts. In either case, the poor, the old and the sick typically make up the greatest proportion of IDP populations, which are therefore of great humanitarian concern.

In contrast to refugees, the international community has no mandate to support IDPs. There is no specialist UN agency and no binding international agreement offering them protection. Since the end of the

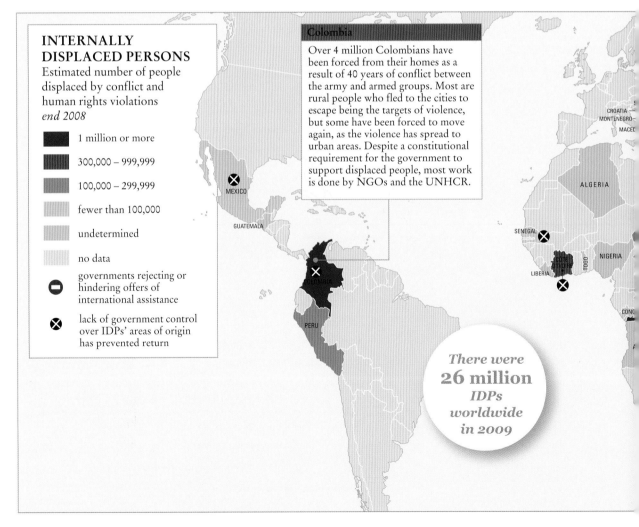

INTERNALLY DISPLACED PERSONS

Estimated number of people displaced by conflict and human rights violations
end 2008

- 1 million or more
- 300,000 – 999,999
- 100,000 – 299,999
- fewer than 100,000
- undetermined
- no data
- ⊖ governments rejecting or hindering offers of international assistance
- ⊗ lack of government control over IDPs' areas of origin has prevented return

Colombia

Over 4 million Colombians have been forced from their homes as a result of 40 years of conflict between the army and armed groups. Most are rural people who fled to the cities to escape being the targets of violence, but some have been forced to move again, as the violence has spread to urban areas. Despite a constitutional requirement for the government to support displaced people, most work is done by NGOs and the UNHCR.

MEXICO

GUATEMALA

COLOMBIA

PERU

CROATIA
MONTENEGRO
MACED

ALGERIA

SENEGAL

NIGERIA

LIBERIA

TOGO

CONG

There were
26 million
IDPs
worldwide
in 2009

1980s, UNHCR has supported IDPs in an ad hoc manner, in addition to its usual focus on refugees, but it was only in 2008 that it set out an explicit objective to support IDPs where possible. Such support always depends on agreement from the government of the country concerned, and since the government is likely to have played at least some role in their initial displacement, such agreement is not always forthcoming. In 1998, the UN's Special Representative on the Human Rights of IDPs began promoting a series of Guiding Principles on Internal Displacement, which form the core of attempts to engage with states, and have been influential in national legislation since then.

Records of IDP numbers tend to include only individuals fleeing conflict, which associates them with refugees. However, individuals may be displaced within their countries for a number of other reasons, which often overlap: large development projects such as dams or roads, environmental disasters or land degradation.

The Three Gorges Dam project on the Yangtze River in China had led to the relocation of 1.27 million people by 2009, including the residents of Old Fengdu, who were relocated to New Fengdu.

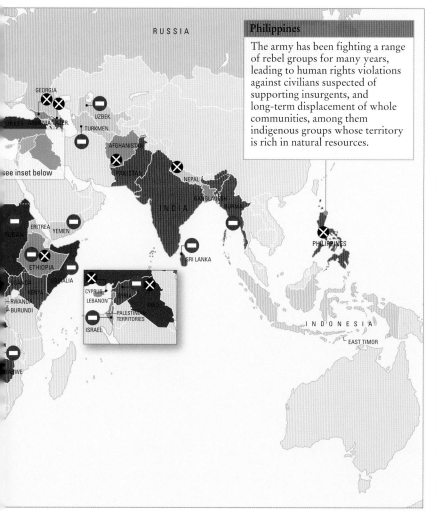

Philippines

The army has been fighting a range of rebel groups for many years, leading to human rights violations against civilians suspected of supporting insurgents, and long-term displacement of whole communities, among them indigenous groups whose territory is rich in natural resources.

Annual floods in Bangladesh typically cover between a third and two-thirds of the country, and result in millions of people being temporarily displaced from their homes.

The Indian Ocean tsunami of December 2004 resulted in the displacement of more than 1.2 million people. In Aceh, Indonesia, recovery was complicated by ongoing conflict, and people were still living in camps more than a year later.

CLIMATE CHANGE

Climate change is likely to result in large movements of people, although maybe over relatively short distances.

The potential impact of climate change on migration has become a major area of debate, with international organizations and charities pointing to the likelihood that a large number of people will be forced to move by sea-level rise and changing rainfall patterns. Estimates range from 200 million to as many as 1 billion affected people by 2050. Yet, projections of the number of "climate refugees" remain highly contested, with the 2007 report of the Intergovernmental Panel on Climate Change resisting the temptation to specify a figure.

Flooding as a result of sea-level rise and increased storm hazards is clearly a major concern in the world's low-elevation coastal zones. Most climate models predict that tropical storms are likely to increase in intensity as the world gets warmer. Hurricane Katrina in the Gulf of Mexico in 2005 demonstrates how a single extreme event can cause considerable population displacement. Around 1.3 million people left New Orleans as the storm approached, and many never returned. Figures for the following year show an outward migration from Louisiana of 250,000 more people than migrated annually prior to the hurricane. The disaster affected social classes differently. Poor people were generally less able to leave the city, and those who did found it more difficult to return.

Up to 70,000 inhabitants of New Orleans were unable to flee before Hurricane Katrina hit in August 2005, and most of those who remained had to fend for themselves. Displacement may not, in fact, be the worst outcome for those who live in areas vulnerable to climate change.

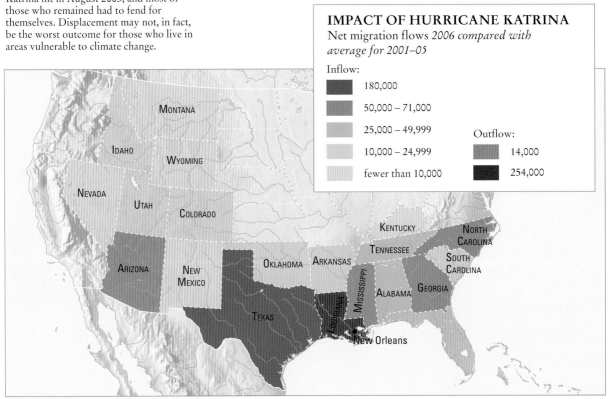

IMPACT OF HURRICANE KATRINA
Net migration flows *2006 compared with average for 2001–05*

Inflow:
- 180,000
- 50,000 – 71,000
- 25,000 – 49,999
- 10,000 – 24,999
- fewer than 10,000

Outflow:
- 14,000
- 254,000

While climate change could increase pressure for people to leave affected areas, questions remain about where affected populations will migrate to, and what factors may facilitate or hinder their migration. It is likely that much migration associated with climate change will be relatively short-distance. Decreasing rainfall and devastating droughts in the Sahel region of Africa during the last three decades of the 20th century led to a series of poor harvests. Rather than encouraging migration, this tended to limit the ability of households to invest in long-distance movement. Instead, larger numbers of poorer people, and especially women, moved to nearby towns during drought periods, with many returning after the rains. Similarly, although millions of people in Bangladesh are left homeless each year due to flooding, most travel very short distances, and try to return and rebuild their houses after the disaster.

Migration rates in most small islands are already high due to poor local employment prospects, but whilst in the short-term climate change is unlikely to have a significant marginal impact on migration, catastrophic flooding could leave some islands and even island states uninhabitable within the next 20 to 30 years.

Around 50 percent of Vietnam's rice is produced in low-lying paddy fields at the mouth of the Mekong Delta.

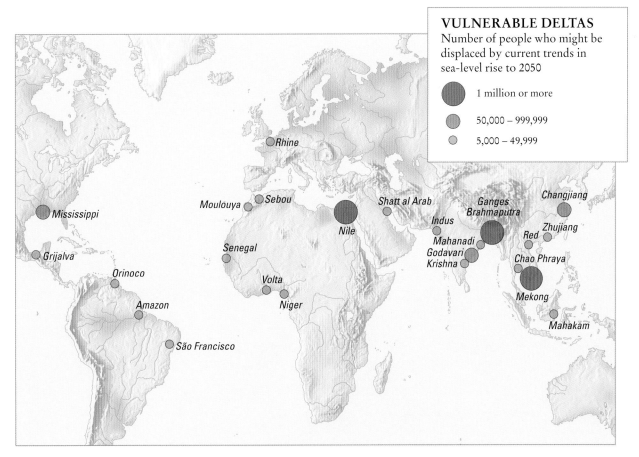

VULNERABLE DELTAS
Number of people who might be displaced by current trends in sea-level rise to 2050

⬤ 1 million or more

● 50,000 – 999,999

• 5,000 – 49,999

Rhine

Mouloua Sebou Shatt al Arab Ganges Brahmaputra Changjiang

Mississippi Nile Indus Zhujiang

Grijalva Senegal Mahanadi Red

Godavari Krishna Chao Phraya

Orinoco Volta

Amazon Niger Mekong

São Francisco Mahakam

IRREGULAR MIGRATION

Irregular migrants are especially vulnerable to traffickers, and coordinated international action is needed to tackle the problem.

Irregular migrants include those crossing international borders without the correct documentation, those remaining in a country beyond the approved duration of stay, and those working in a country without necessary authorization. They are obviously keen to remain hidden, and it is therefore difficult to be precise about their numbers.

It is increasingly difficult for people from poorer countries to gain access to wealthy ones, and would-be migrants often pay for assistance. This may be from individuals offering help with crossing a particular border, or from transnational criminal organizations, who arrange complex international journeys, in exchange for which migrants are committed to working for the organization as a way of paying the huge fees it charges. Such assistance is usually labelled either smuggling, or trafficking (which involves some form of coercion or deception).

The welfare states of Europe have gradually excluded irregular migrants from all forms of publicly provided social provision, such as healthcare. Efforts are now increasingly targeted at migrants before they

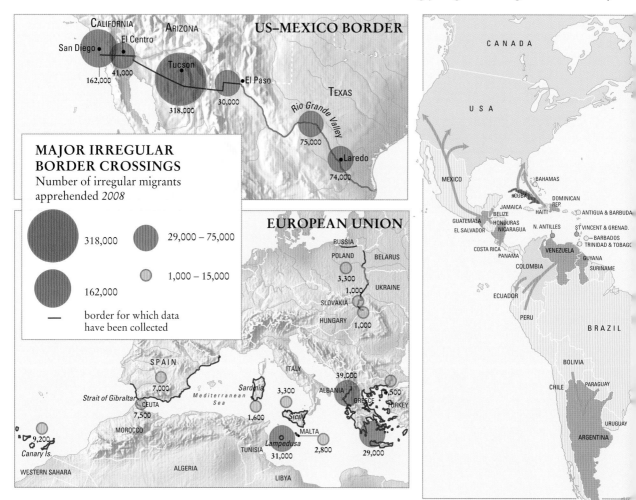

US–MEXICO BORDER

CALIFORNIA
ARIZONA
El Centro
San Diego •
Tucson
41,000
162,000
318,000
• El Paso
30,000
TEXAS
Rio Grande Valley
75,000
• Laredo
74,000

MAJOR IRREGULAR BORDER CROSSINGS
Number of irregular migrants apprehended *2008*

318,000

29,000 – 75,000

1,000 – 15,000

162,000

— border for which data have been collected

EUROPEAN UNION

RUSSIA
POLAND
BELARUS
3,300
1,000
UKRAINE
SLOVAKIA
HUNGARY
1,000
SPAIN
ITALY
39,000
Sardinia
3,300
ALBANIA
1,500
7,000
Strait of Gibraltar
CEUTA
GREECE
TURKEY
Mediterranean Sea
7,500
MOROCCO
1,600
Sicily
9,200
Canary Is.
TUNISIA
Lampedusa
31,000
MALTA
2,800
29,000
WESTERN SAHARA
ALGERIA
LIBYA

CANADA
U S A
MEXICO
BAHAMAS
CUBA
DOMINICAN REP.
JAMAICA
HAITI
ANTIGUA & BARBUDA
GUATEMALA
BELIZE
ST VINCENT & GRENAD.
EL SALVADOR
HONDURAS
NICARAGUA
N. ANTILLES
BARBADOS
TRINIDAD & TOBAGO
COSTA RICA
VENEZUELA
GUYANA
PANAMA
COLOMBIA
SURINAME
ECUADOR
PERU
BRAZIL
BOLIVIA
CHILE
PARAGUAY
URUGUAY
ARGENTINA

attempt to gain entry. Figures on people apprehended making irregular border crossings not only provide information on the number of migrants, but also on the resources devoted to migration control. Such data are only made publicly available by the US Department of Homeland Security, and the European border control organization Frontex, which are responsible for the most controlled border areas in the world.

The human rights imperative to prevent the forced labour associated with trafficking has inevitably blurred with security and border control concerns. Anti-trafficking has become a powerful political force, most clearly demonstrated by the annual Trafficking in Persons reports issued by the US State Department, which classify countries according to their support for anti-trafficking measures. Those in the lowest category for two consecutive years face withdrawal of support by the USA, with significant financial consequences.

TRAFFICKING

Compliance with
US Trafficking Victims
Protection Act (TVPA)
2009

fully complies with minimum standards established by TVPA

does not fully comply but is making significant efforts to do so

does not fully comply, is making significant efforts but there is still evidence of severe forms of trafficking

does not fully comply

selected major routes for irregular migration

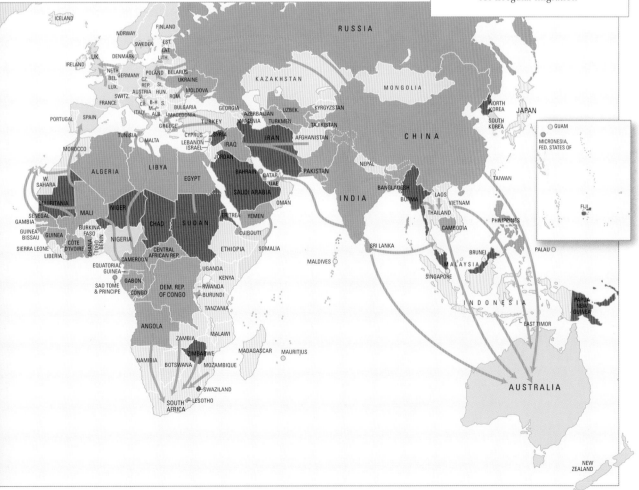

DEATH AT THE BORDER

The number of migrants who die while trying to evade border controls is a humanitarian crisis.

The number of irregular migrants who lose their lives during attempts to reach their desired destinations is one of the most shocking aspects of the international migration system. It is, of course, impossible to know how many migrants die under these circumstances since the bodies of migrants who drown at sea or who expire on long desert crossings may never be found. Even approximate statistics are only available for the world's most policed borders. An estimated 5,600 migrants have died attempting to cross the US–Mexico border in the 15 years since the US border patrol's Operation Gatekeeper began in 1994. The figure in Europe is even higher: probably more than 10,000 for the same period. Elsewhere, there is no basis to support estimates, but across the Sahara desert, the Gulf of Aden, and in the open oceans around Australia and South-East Asia, fatalities are undoubtedly high.

The increasing severity of border controls to wealthy countries is often cited as an explanation for the high number of fatalities. Migration controls are increasingly coordinated at European level through the EU and the largely overlapping Schengen system. The EU also coordinates border control activities with neighbouring

CAUSE OF DEATH
Of irregular migrants trying to enter Europe
2006–09

Total number of deaths: 2,103

suffocation 1%
violence 2%
accidental injury 2%
starvation/ exposure 9%
drowning 86%

EUROPEAN BORDER DEATHS
2006–09

- countries in European Union and/or Schengen Agreement
- EU candidate countries
- European Neighbourhood Policy partners
- not party to European border agreements

Number of recorded deaths of irregular migrants trying to enter Europe

- 300 – 702
- 138 – 193
- 1 – 30

countries partly through the rules of acceding to the EU for a small number of accession countries, and partly through the European Neighbourhood Policy.

In a small number of cases, border control forces are directly responsible for the deaths of migrants. More significant is the displacement factor as migrants seek out the least controlled parts of the border, which are often the most hostile. On the US–Mexico border, it is the remote desert of the Tucson sector which claims the most lives, and in Europe long, hazardous journeys by sea offer a way around the intense monitoring of shorter stretches such as across the Strait of Gibraltar. Yet, border controls are not the only explanation. In fact, it is increasingly common for border control agents to come to the assistance of migrants in distress.

Another common explanation for the high number of deaths is that migrants are not aware of the dangers of irregular migration, but research shows that this is not the case either. The fundamental driver of these extremely risky migrations is increasing global inequalities, generating a search for opportunities which the predominantly young, male migrants are persistently denied at home.

Border death memorial on the 14-mile border fence between Tijuana, Mexico and San Diego, California. It records the number of people who, deterred by the barrier, have died attempting to enter the USA across the desert.

US–MEXICO BORDER DEATHS
Number of recorded deaths of irregular migrants trying to enter USA
2008
by border patrol sector

● 171

● 20 – 97   ● 3 – 8

——— new barrier authorized by US Border Fence Act (2006)

——— Border Patrol section

A separation barrier already exists along a fifth of the 3,140 km (1,950 mile) Mexico–US border, and the US Border Fence Act (2006) specified an extension of these barriers. The focus is on the creation of a "virtual fence" – a system of radar, underground sensors, cameras and watch towers.

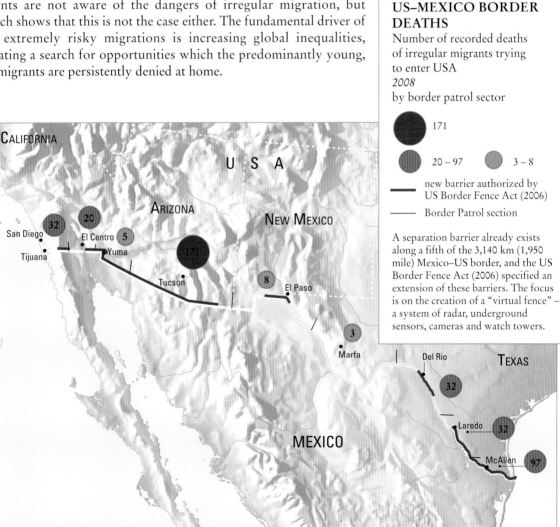

MIGRATION & GENDER

Where people migrate to and from, the jobs they do, and roles they play tend to be influenced by their gender.

Most emigrations start as a migration of young adult males, followed by family migration as the migration stream matures, and conditions for settlement improve. If the emigration and immigration rules allow it, and if labour market conditions in the origin and destination countries are favourable, single unaccompanied female migration may follow. A good example of this "feminization" of a migration stream is the Philippines.

Before about 1990, the emigration flow from the Philippines consisted largely of single men, but in 2006, 59 percent of land-based Filipino workers given new contracts to work overseas were female, while additional women travelled as spouses of workers, or as international marriage migrants. Female labour migrants tend to predominate among migrants from the more rural north and south of the country. In many cases, they form part of a "care chain", working as carers in the country of immigration, while their own children are looked after by other family members back in the Philippines. In addition to anxieties about the effects of family separation on

ORIGIN AND GENDER OF MIGRANTS FROM PHILIPPINES

Those who departed overseas *2003–08* and worked abroad during *2008*

male — female

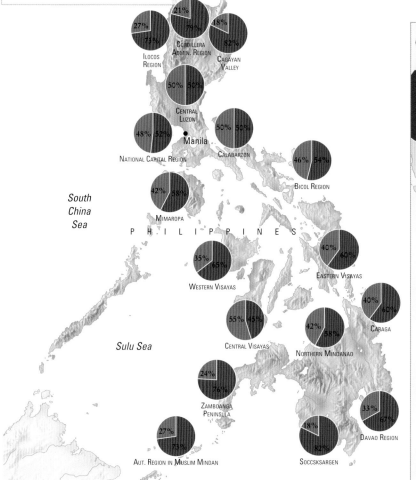

marriage stability and child development, human rights organizations have been concerned that far too many female Filipino workers have been subjected to exploitation and abuse, especially in the Middle East, and in South-East and East Asia.

While many sending countries have reluctantly accepted the inevitability of a loss of population (often of their brightest and best) through international migration, the Philippines government has positively encouraged such emigration. Men work as ships' crews, and on construction sites and in factories in many countries of the world, while women form a large part of the international migration of nurses, care assistants and domestic helpers. Despite the enormous remittances this has brought to the Philippines economy (over $1 billion per month), it has failed as a development strategy. While other South-East Asian countries have greatly increased their wealth and stability over the last 50 years, the Philippines continues to be dragged down by poverty, political corruption and separatist conflict.

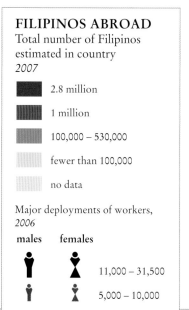

FILIPINOS ABROAD

Total number of Filipinos estimated in country
2007

	2.8 million
	1 million
	100,000 – 530,000
	fewer than 100,000
	no data

Major deployments of workers, 2006

males   females

11,000 – 31,500

5,000 – 10,000

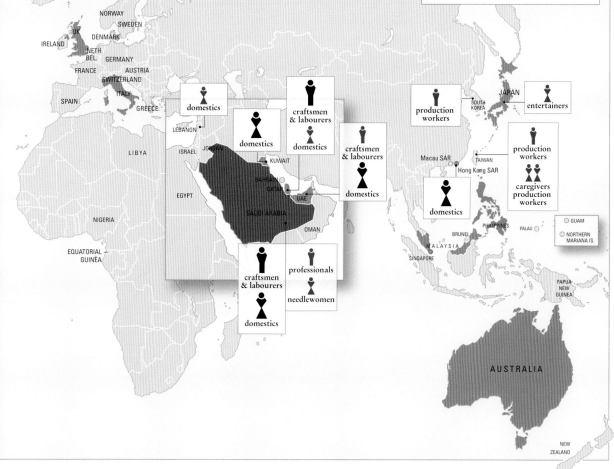

MIGRATION FOR MARRIAGE

International marriage migration is filling the gap in rural communities left by migration to the cities.

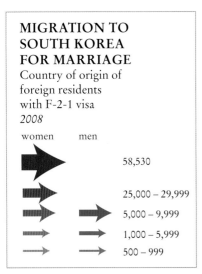

MIGRATION TO SOUTH KOREA FOR MARRIAGE

Country of origin of foreign residents with F-2-1 visa
2008

women   men

58,530

25,000 – 29,999

5,000 – 9,999

1,000 – 5,999

500 – 999

With increasing globalization, marriages between people of different nationalities are on the increase. One partner in the marriage will usually become a migrant in the other person's country. Where the partners, and the countries from which they originate, are relatively equal in status and wealth, social exclusion and individual exploitation may be avoided. But, all too often, power relations are unequal, and the person from a less advantaged background or country suffers abuse. Race and ethnicity, exacerbated by social stereotyping and nationalism, differences in language and religion, can compound the problem, making the partner who carries the less-valued culture vulnerable to discrimination and harassment. In high-income, patriarchal societies, the position of immigrant wives from developing countries can be particularly dire.

South Korea has only recently become a country of immigration and, even more recently, a country of international marriage migration. There has been a major increase in the number of international marriages, some of them brought about with the help of commercial dating agencies. Of the 854,000 registered foreign residents in Korea, 122,000 (14 percent) hold an F-2-1 visa, entitling them to marry a Korean. About half of these are from China, of whom over half are *Joseonjok* – ethnic Koreans, who also partly account for the flow from Uzbekistan. Only a small number come from developed countries such as Japan, the USA, and Canada.

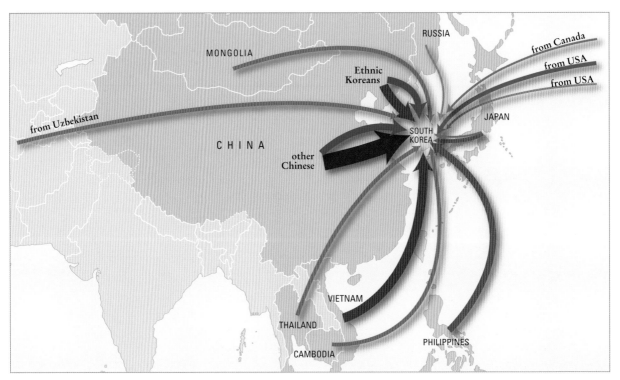

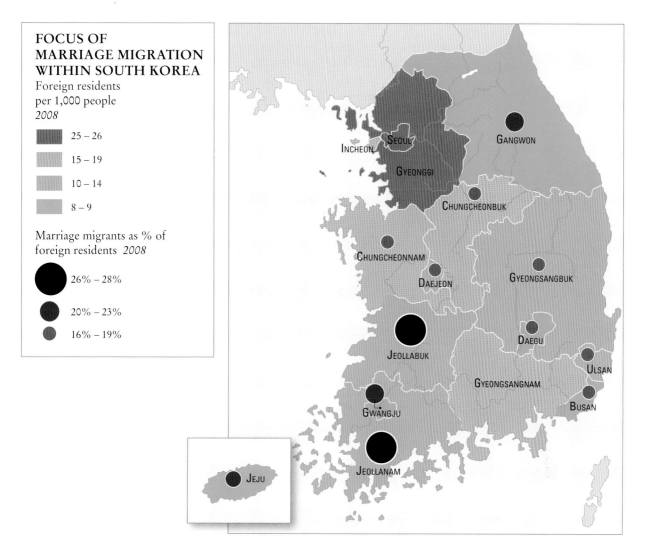

FOCUS OF
MARRIAGE MIGRATION
WITHIN SOUTH KOREA

Foreign residents
per 1,000 people
2008

- 25 – 26
- 15 – 19
- 10 – 14
- 8 – 9

Marriage migrants as % of
foreign residents *2008*

- 26% – 28%
- 20% – 23%
- 16% – 19%

The gender balance of spouses is related to the degree of development. The large majority of marriage migrants are women from poor countries, the minority are men from rich ones.

The distribution of international marriage migrants within Korea is very revealing. While the vast majority of foreign residents are to be found in the Seoul metropolitan region, and in the industrialized countryside around and to the south of the city, international marriage migrants make up a larger proportion of foreign residents in the rural, and relatively remote, areas of the country. This reflects the fact that male farmers in rapidly developing countries often have difficulty finding local marriage partners. Young adult women in rural areas tend to migrate to the cities, seeking independence and career development, modern lifestyles and bright social prospects. International marriage migrants fill the gap.

CHILD MIGRATION

Child migrants are largely uncounted and unstudied, and therefore ignored by policy makers.

Children almost certainly make up a significant proportion of migrants worldwide, yet studies of contemporary migration are often focused on adults, either ignoring the movement of children, or assuming that it is subsidiary to that of adults. Children do move with their parents, but they also move independently, in search of work and education. In some cases they are trafficked, or subjected to violence and/or exploitative working conditions, but this is far from being the norm in either developed or developing countries.

There is no global estimate of the volume of child migration, whether with parents or independently, although there is information on specific countries. Up to 4 percent of the 35 million children in Argentina, Chile and South Africa are estimated to be migrants. Many of these have moved independently of their parents: up to 250,000 between provinces within the countries, and up to 20,000 internationally.

International migrants in Ghana include a much higher proportion of children than in the general population, possibly reflecting the common practice amongst Ghanaians abroad of sending children back to live with extended family members, or attend school. Mexico also has a high proportion of children amongst its migrants, but in the Philippines and South Africa, migrants of all kinds (internal and international) are much less likely to be children.

Migration affects children in a range of ways. The fact that children migrate with their families can have significant consequences for public policy, particularly if their parents' migration is undocumented. For example, planning decisions on allocation of school expenditure may be based on erroneous calculations of where children are living. If children are left behind by parents who migrate, there are concerns for their emotional well-being and psychological development, even if those children might benefit substantially from remittances that are invested in schooling, health, housing and consumption more generally.

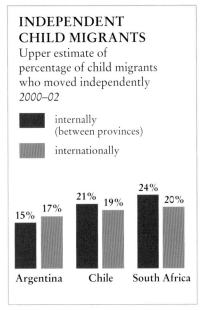

INDEPENDENT CHILD MIGRANTS

Upper estimate of percentage of child migrants who moved independently
2000–02

- internally (between provinces)
- internationally

Argentina: 15% / 17%
Chile: 21% / 19%
South Africa: 24% / 20%

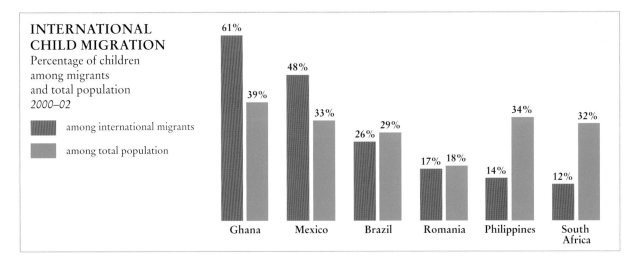

INTERNATIONAL CHILD MIGRATION

Percentage of children among migrants and total population
2000–02

- among international migrants
- among total population

Ghana: 61% / 39%
Mexico: 48% / 33%
Brazil: 26% / 29%
Romania: 17% / 18%
Philippines: 14% / 34%
South Africa: 12% / 32%

The autonomous migration of children is the most contentious policy area. In Ghana, the migration of young boys and girls from poor parts of the rural north to cities such as Accra and Kumasi is a matter of considerable concern for policy makers, and often leads to these children living on the streets, working for low wages, and being subject to violence and exploitation.

Yet, such children who migrate independently of their parents or of adult guardians are in many ways seeking similar social and economic opportunities to those of adult migrants. Many leave rural areas because of the few educational or employment opportunities on offer. Some – notably in South Africa – leave because they have lost one or both parents. The fact that they are usually not acknowledged as migrants means that "solutions" to their situation too often focus on preventing their migration, or returning them to their home areas, rather than on supporting them in the strategies they have chosen, or seeking to provide them with protection in the places in which they are living.

AGE AT FIRST MIGRATION

Of young Ghanaian North–South migrants surveyed in Accra and Kumasi
2005

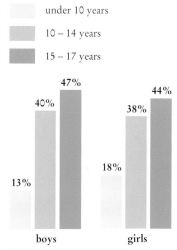

YOUNG MIGRANTS IN GHANA

2005

net inflow of child migrants

net outflow of child migrants

Origins of young North–South migrants in markets in Accra and Kumasi

→ to Accra
→ to Kumasi

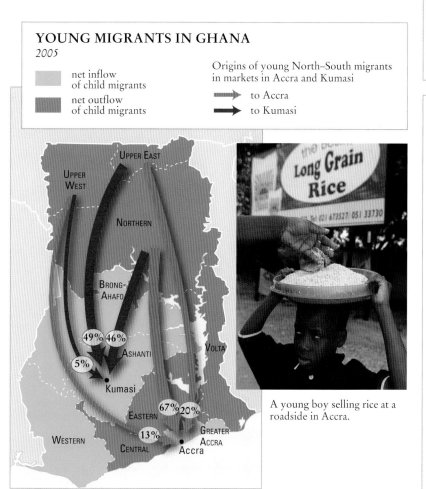

A young boy selling rice at a roadside in Accra.

OCCUPATION

Of young Ghanaian North–South migrants surveyed in Accra and Kumasi
2005

porter/truck pusher

technician/mechanic

street vendor

trading/selling

other

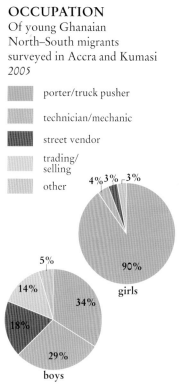

STUDENT MIGRATION

Student migration is an important precursor to skilled migration.

The crossing of borders by people seeking education, while representing only 2 percent of total international movement, is increasing in importance. A growing number of graduates are being given the right to remain in their host country to augment that country's skills base.

In 2006, 2.7 million people were pursuing higher education outside their own country. Just under half were studying in the major English-speaking countries of the world, with over one-fifth in the USA. This internationalization of education has been ascribed to the perceived benefit that competence in the English language brings to those wishing to participate fully in the global economy. Nevertheless, a significant number of foreign students are being educated in French, German, Russian, Chinese, Japanese, and Arabic institutes of higher learning.

The migration of students is part of globalization, but only the USA and the UK have truly global student populations. Students travelling to

ORIGINS
Region of origin of students going to major destination countries
2006

Total: 2.0 million

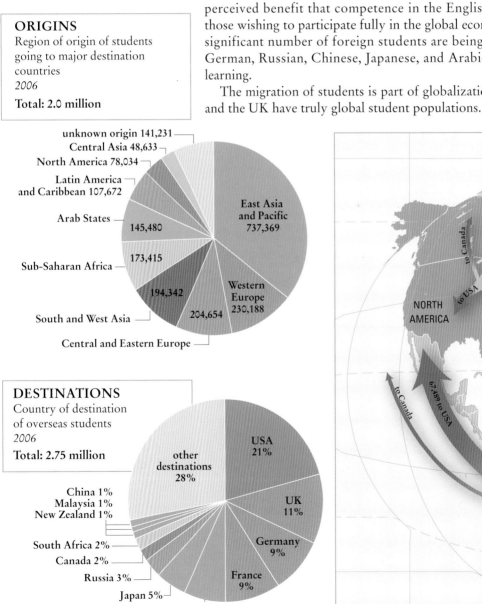

unknown origin 141,231
Central Asia 48,633
North America 78,034
Latin America and Caribbean 107,672
Arab States — 145,480
Sub-Saharan Africa — 173,415
South and West Asia — 194,342
Central and Eastern Europe — 204,654
East Asia and Pacific 737,369
Western Europe 230,188

DESTINATIONS
Country of destination of overseas students
2006

Total: 2.75 million

USA 21%
other destinations 28%
China 1%
Malaysia 1%
New Zealand 1%
South Africa 2%
Canada 2%
Russia 3%
Japan 5%
Australia 7%
France 9%
Germany 9%
UK 11%

to Canada
to USA
to UK
to Australia
NORTH AMERICA
to UK
to France
to Germany
to Canada
67,489 to USA
LATIN AMERICA AND CARIBBEAN

Australia and Japan come primarily from other parts of Asia. Although over 60 percent of students to the USA come from Asia, Europeans and Latin Americans also figure prominently.

Students are obviously attracted to the principal centres of learning in developed countries, such as Oxford and Cambridge in the UK, and the Ivy League universities in the USA, but most universities in the developed world are facing a declining number of home-grown students. They are therefore seeking not only to admit more international students, but to establish joint programmes with universities overseas – even to build complete branch campuses in countries such as the United Arab Emirates, China, and Malaysia. Developing countries, too, are rapidly expanding their tertiary education, and developed-country institutes of higher learning will soon be in direct competition with centres of excellence in Singapore, Hong Kong, Shanghai, Beijing, Mumbai, and Delhi.

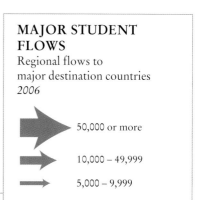

MAJOR STUDENT FLOWS

Regional flows to major destination countries
2006

50,000 or more

10,000 – 49,999

5,000 – 9,999

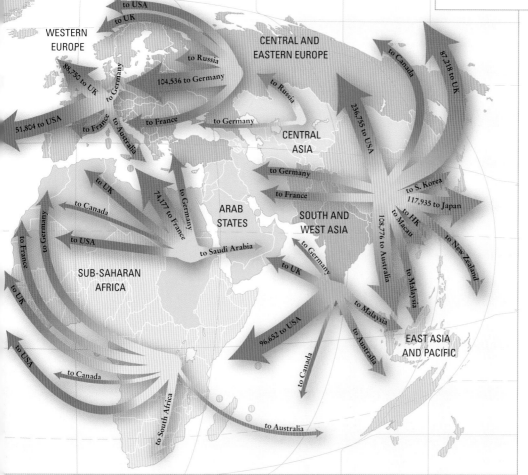

SKILLED MIGRATION

Emigrants are among the more educated and skilled people in their country of origin, although not necessarily in their country of destination.

In immigration statistics, the "skilled" – those with tertiary-level education – make up a category of immigration. The majority of developed economies seek to reduce the number of unskilled migrants, and to use immigration programmes to increase the number of skilled migrants to fill specific job requirements, particularly in the fields of health and information technology. Skilled migrants adapt more easily to destination societies, and tend to be looked upon more positively by the citizens of receiving countries than are unskilled migrants.

Globally, the skilled represent a minority of total migrants, but one that is increasing. The proportion of the skilled in annual immigration flows to the USA and Europe increased markedly during the 1990s. Skilled migrants originate primarily in developed economies and in a relatively small number of middle-income developing countries, such as China, India, Mexico and the Philippines. It is in these countries that

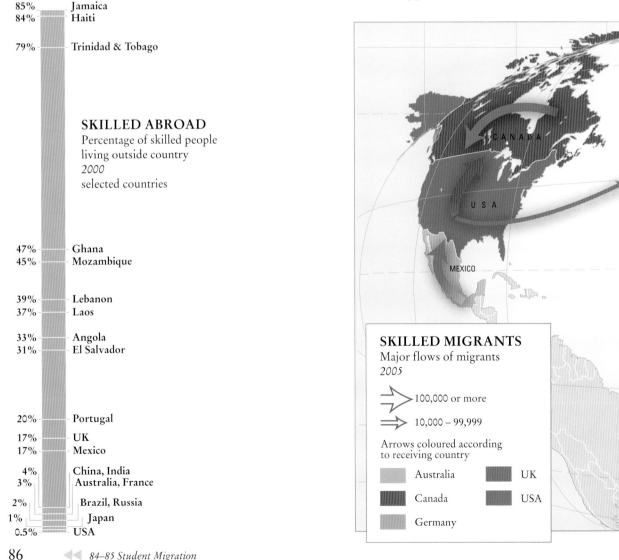

SKILLED ABROAD
Percentage of skilled people living outside country
2000
selected countries

- 85% Jamaica
- 84% Haiti
- 79% Trinidad & Tobago
- 47% Ghana
- 45% Mozambique
- 39% Lebanon
- 37% Laos
- 33% Angola
- 31% El Salvador
- 20% Portugal
- 17% UK
- 17% Mexico
- 4% China, India
- 3% Australia, France
- 2% Brazil, Russia
- 1% Japan
- 0.5% USA

SKILLED MIGRANTS
Major flows of migrants
2005

→ 100,000 or more

⇒ 10,000 – 99,999

Arrows coloured according to receiving country

- Australia
- Canada
- Germany
- UK
- USA

the institutions to train the skilled are found. Evidence of a negative impact of a "brain drain" is difficult to find for these economies. Some, such as the Philippines, specifically train nurses for the global market.

At least 20 small and weak economies, most of which are islands, have more skilled workers beyond their borders than within, although many of these people have left their country specifically to be trained. While skilled workers tend to return to their country of origin when something exists for them to return to – as has occurred with dynamic economies of East Asia from North America, Australasia and Europe – where there are no prospects at home, workers will remain abroad. Programmes that use the skills of those abroad to benefit their home country are being developed both by national and international organizations. Some invite the skilled to return home to provide training, or to investigate investment opportunities.

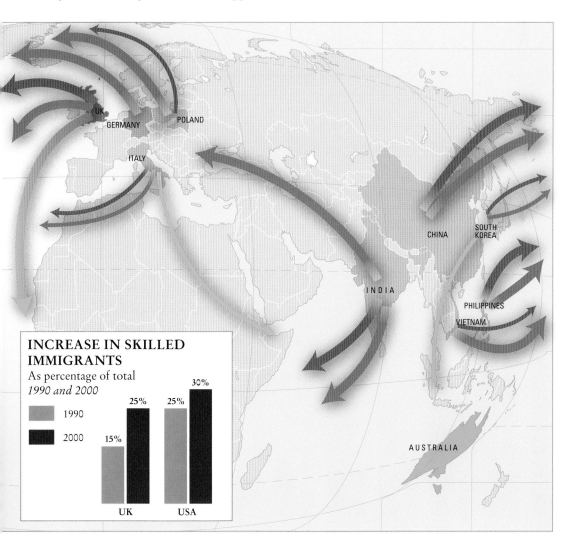

INCREASE IN SKILLED IMMIGRANTS
As percentage of total
1990 and 2000

1990
2000

UK: 15% / 25%
USA: 25% / 30%

INTERNATIONAL RETIREMENT

Retirement migration is driven by migrants from rich countries seeking a more attractive lifestyle.

International retirement migration is mainly a European phenomenon, with the flow primarily from Northern Europe to the Mediterranean South. The majority of migrants come from the UK and Germany, but some come from Scandinavia, the Netherlands and Belgium. Most retire to Spain and Italy, but Portugal, Greece, Cyprus and Malta are also established retirement destinations. France and Switzerland both send and receive international retirees.

In the USA, most long-distance retirement moves are internal, from the cold north to "sunshine states" such as Florida and California, although growing numbers look to Mexico and further south. Retirement migration can be either seasonal – so-called "snowbirds" – or involve permanent settlement in warmer climes.

Several factors stimulate the growth of retirement migration. Demographic change is leading to an increase in the proportion of older people, while economic factors – rising incomes, pensions, savings and inherited wealth – have enabled more people of retirement age to think about moving abroad, where property and the cost of living are cheaper. Education, knowledge of language, and past holiday experiences have all made potential retirees more aware of the attractions of such a move – either to a coastal location, such as one of the Spanish "costas", or to an attractive rural setting such as the Dordogne in France, or Tuscany in Italy. Finally, underpinning all is geography and climate, as warm dry weather enables a healthier, more relaxed outdoor lifestyle.

While UK pension records indicate a significant number of pensioners in Spain, they also reflect historical migration patterns, including British migration to North America and Australasia, and inflows of migrants to the UK from ex-colonial countries, and from Europe. Some pensioners appear to be joining their emigrant children, or to be returning to their family roots.

Retirement abroad does carry risks, however, especially if it is to a country with a different language, culture and health system. Difficult decisions have to be made when illness strikes, physical mobility is lost, or a partner dies. Changes in currency exchange rates and a fall in property prices can leave pensioners abroad in straightened economic circumstances. Such personal and financial crises impel some retirement migrants to move back to their home countries, where they may also encounter problems if they have little to return to, except the end of a dream.

The number of over-65s in the USA is forecast to **double** *between 2000 and 2030*

PENSIONERS ABROAD

Largest overseas populations of recipients of UK pensions
2002 & 2008

- 2002
- 2008

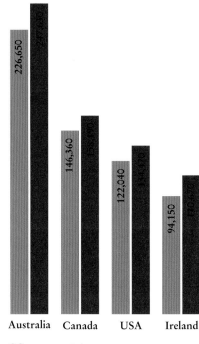

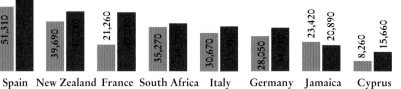

226,650	146,360	122,040	94,150	51,310	39,690	21,260	35,270	30,670	28,050 23,420	20,890	8,260 15,660
Australia	Canada	USA	Ireland	Spain	New Zealand	France	South Africa	Italy	Germany	Jamaica	Cyprus

FOREIGN PENSIONERS IN SPAIN

Foreigners aged 65 years and over
as percentage of population of province
aged 65 years and over *2001*

Number of foreigners
aged 65 years and over:

10.1%

7.9%

1.9% – 5.2%

0.6% – 1.0%

0.5% or less

4,800 – 23,660,
country of origin shown

1,000 – 3,000

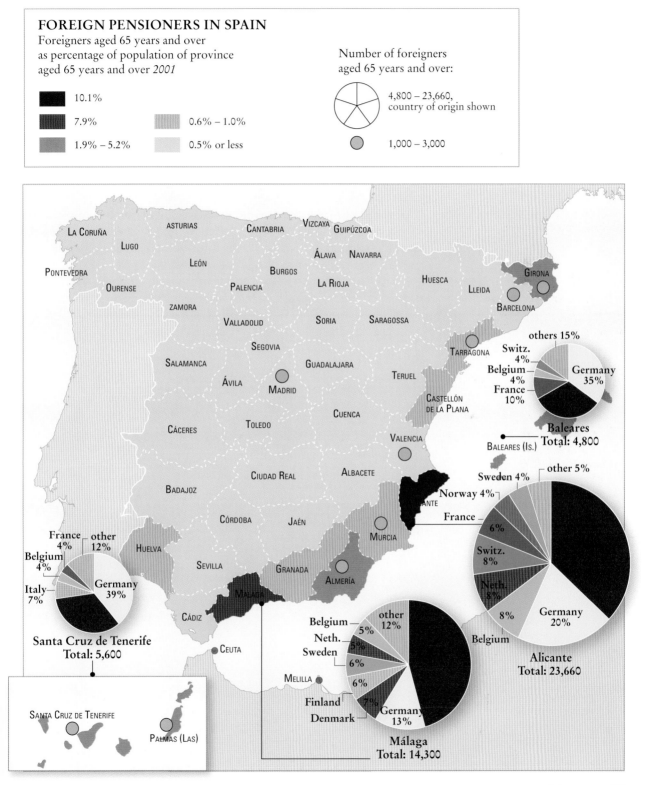

others 15%
Switz. 4%
Belgium 4%
France 10%
Germany 35%
Baleares
Total: 4,800

Sweden 4%
other 5%
Norway 4%
France 6%
Switz. 8%
Neth. 8%
Belgium 8%
Germany 20%
Alicante
Total: 23,660

France 4%
Belgium 4%
other 12%
Italy 7%
Germany 39%
Santa Cruz de Tenerife
Total: 5,600

Belgium 5%
Neth. 5%
Sweden 6%
other 12%
Finland 6%
Denmark 7%
Germany 13%
Málaga
Total: 14,300

Santa Cruz de Tenerife

Palmas (Las)

RETURN MIGRATION

Many migrants intend to return, and those who do so can benefit their native country.

Migration is not simply a one-way event, from origin to destination. Many people, either on the point of departure, or when living abroad, state their intention to return. Some are contracted to do so, but, because of the paucity of statistics, it is difficult to estimate what proportion of the remainder realize their intention. What is clear, however, is that a significant number do make the return journey.

Migrants return for a number of reasons. Some, known as "target migrants", return when they have earned a certain sum of money or gained a qualification. Others return for economic reasons: because the economy of their home countries has improved, or because of unemployment in the host countries. Although the global economic crisis of 2008–09 caused the return migration of some workers, there is little evidence of mass returns. Returns are also driven by personal and family motives, such as nostalgia, failure to integrate, desire to bring up children in the home country, need to look after ageing parents, or migrants' own retirement back to their "native soil".

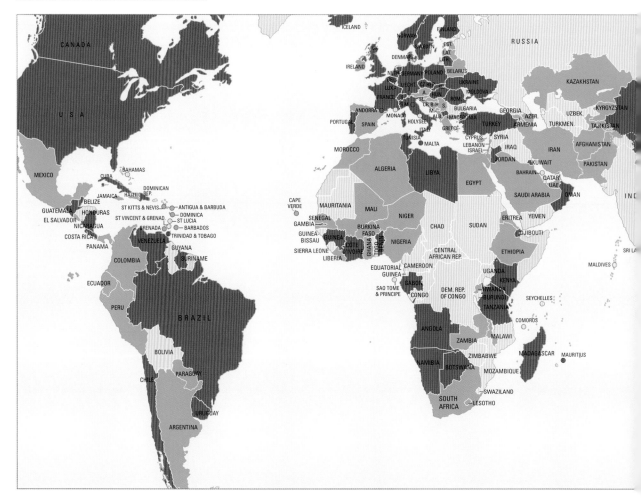

Return and reintegration may not be smooth, and many become nostalgic for their country of emigration. "Successful" returnees may be the object of jealousy on the part of non-migrants, whereas "failures" are pitied and rejected. On the other hand, innovative returnees may stimulate development in their home countries by investing in businesses, or by introducing more progressive ideas about politics, health, education, or gender relations. For this reason, many countries have policies that encourage return from their migrant diasporas.

While some returnees go back to their villages of origin, many prefer, or are constrained, to return to larger towns and cities which offer better employment and social opportunities. Italy – one of the few countries to publish detailed regional return statistics – illustrates this. During the post-war decades of mass emigration (mainly between the late 1940s and the early 1970s) most left from the rural south, while there were relatively more returnees (mainly between the late 1960s and the early 1980s) to northern regions, centres of industry and urban development.

Emigrants

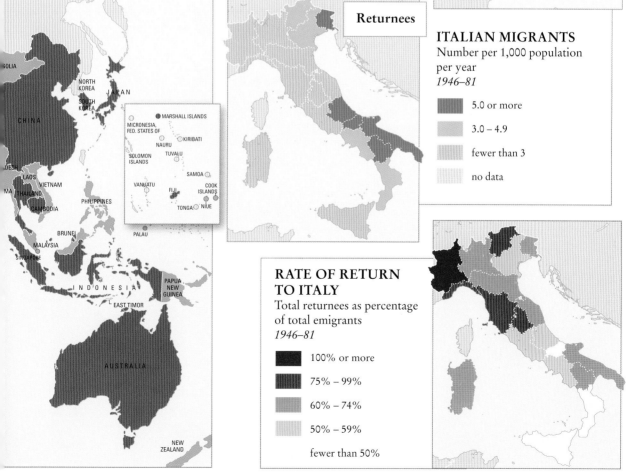

Returnees

ITALIAN MIGRANTS
Number per 1,000 population per year
1946–81

- 5.0 or more
- 3.0 – 4.9
- fewer than 3
- no data

RATE OF RETURN TO ITALY
Total returnees as percentage of total emigrants
1946–81

- 100% or more
- 75% – 99%
- 60% – 74%
- 50% – 59%
- fewer than 50%

MIGRATION & INTEGRATION

The extent to which immigrant communities are expected to integrate into host cultures varies around the world.

Integration, assimilation, and acculturation are some of the terms used to describe the evolving relationship between immigrants and the society in which they make their home. Integration, like the other two terms, is a contested notion, not least because it implies the superiority of the host society to which the immigrants have to adapt.

There are diverse views and models of integration in different immigrant-receiving countries. Assimilation, where immigrants are supposed, eventually, to become indistinguishable from members of the host society, is associated with the USA and France. Multiculturalism, where migrants are regarded as "minority ethnic communities" and are allowed or encouraged to retain the cultures of their country of origin, is prevalent in Canada, Australia, the Netherlands and the UK. However, recent events – the 2001 riots in towns in the north of England, the July 2005 bombings in London, and in the Netherlands the murders of radical politician Pim Fortuyn (2002) and film-maker Theo van Gogh (2004) – have called into question the multicultural model. This has led to a discourse of "parallel societies", the indigenous on the one hand, and the immigrant, especially the Muslim, on the other. At least in Europe, a swing back to assimilation has occurred, with greater demands on immigrants to learn the host-country language and subscribe to core national values.

Integration and assimilation are not simple linear processes; they are multifaceted, and can progress, or regress, over generations. Whilst, under the classical American model, assimilation is predicted to be complete by the third generation, there is much discussion about the non-assimilation of the second generation which, rather than progressing towards the American "mainstream society", is becoming absorbed into an underclass of poverty, unemployment and street gangs, and staying within ethnic enclaves.

Various dimensions of integration are recognized. Under "structural" integration we can chart immigrants' progress though the education system, in the labour market, and their access to housing. Social and cultural integration involve language, religion, food habits, social relations and intermarriage. Political integration involves voting rights, citizenship and naturalization. There is also a question of identity – whether migrants identify with the host society and feel they "belong".

Finally, there are questions of policy: the extent to which countries encourage immigrants' integration, or put up barriers in the form of legal obstacles to citizenship, naturalization, family reunion, and welfare rights. The Migration and Integration Policy Index (MIPEX) developed by the British Council and the Migration Policy Group allows comparisons of European countries on the basis of "integration performance" measured by six criteria: anti-discrimination measures, the rights to long-term residence, political participation, nationality, and family reunion, and access to the labour market.

EUROPEAN POLICIES ON INTEGRATION

As scored by the
Migrant Integration
Policy Index (MIPEX)
2006

- critically unfavourable
- unfavourable
- slightly unfavourable
- half-way to best practice
- slightly unfavourable
- favourable
- best practice

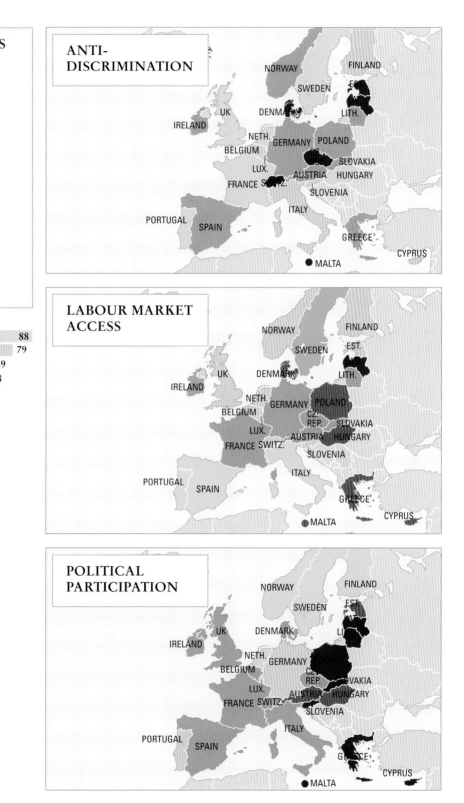

Sweden	88
Portugal	79
Belgium	69
Netherlands	68
Finland	67
Italy	65
Norway	64
UK	63
Spain	61
Slovenia	55
France	55
Luxembourg	55
Germany	53
Ireland	53
Switzerland	50
Hungary	48
Czech Republic	48
Estonia	46
Lithuania	45
Poland	44
Denmark	44
Malta	41
Slovakia	40
Greece	40
Austria	39
Cyprus	39
Latvia	30

OVERALL SCORE

For policies on six aspects
of migrant integration
2006

ANTI-DISCRIMINATION

LABOUR MARKET ACCESS

POLITICAL PARTICIPATION

VOTING FROM ABROAD

Most countries allow their citizens to vote from abroad.

Most countries allow emigrants to vote in national elections. All countries that hold elections allow state employees, such as diplomats or soldiers, posted abroad to participate. More controversial is the extension of this right to all citizens, regardless of their reasons for being out of the country at the time of an election, although in some cases, such as post-conflict elections, it is more commonly accepted.

There are two long-standing objections to allowing emigrants to vote from abroad: that they lack the information necessary to make an informed judgement and that, since they will be unaffected by the consequences of their choice, they cannot be trusted to vote responsibly. Those in favour of extra-territorial voting argue that international communications enable emigrants to make a well-informed choice, and that emigrants often have an important stake in their home country – family, property, remittances, and the possibility of an eventual return. It

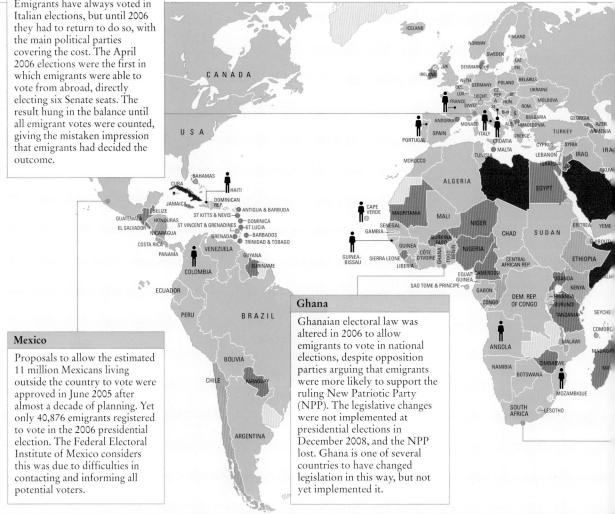

Italy

Emigrants have always voted in Italian elections, but until 2006 they had to return to do so, with the main political parties covering the cost. The April 2006 elections were the first in which emigrants were able to vote from abroad, directly electing six Senate seats. The result hung in the balance until all emigrant votes were counted, giving the mistaken impression that emigrants had decided the outcome.

Mexico

Proposals to allow the estimated 11 million Mexicans living outside the country to vote were approved in June 2005 after almost a decade of planning. Yet only 40,876 emigrants registered to vote in the 2006 presidential election. The Federal Electoral Institute of Mexico considers this was due to difficulties in contacting and informing all potential voters.

Ghana

Ghanaian electoral law was altered in 2006 to allow emigrants to vote in national elections, despite opposition parties arguing that emigrants were more likely to support the ruling New Patriotic Party (NPP). The legislative changes were not implemented at presidential elections in December 2008, and the NPP lost. Ghana is one of several countries to have changed legislation in this way, but not yet implemented it.

is also rare for a country to allow non-citizen residents to vote, so if emigrants without dual citizenship are denied a vote in their country of origin, they will be disenfranchised.

Voting from abroad is now extremely common, and legislative changes to allow it have become more frequent in recent years; Mexico, Italy and South Africa have passed laws since 2003 to allow emigrants to vote without returning. In countries where it has been possible for a long time, such as the USA, it raises few issues. In some countries, however, its introduction has been felt to bestow political advantage on the party in power, and controversy has been intense. There were violent demonstrations on the streets of Accra, Ghana, for example, when legislation to allow emigrants to vote was passed in 2006. In other countries, such as Mozambique, it has been legal practice since 2004, but has yet to be implemented.

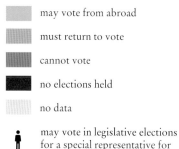

VOTING STATUS
Of people living abroad in relation to elections in their country of citizenship
2008

- may vote from abroad
- must return to vote
- cannot vote
- no elections held
- no data
- may vote in legislative elections for a special representative for people living outside the country

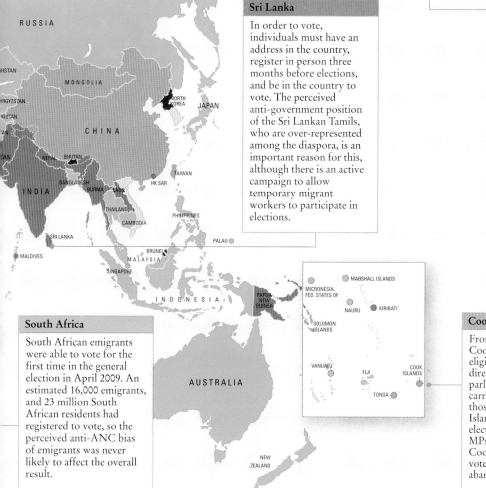

Sri Lanka

In order to vote, individuals must have an address in the country, register in person three months before elections, and be in the country to vote. The perceived anti-government position of the Sri Lankan Tamils, who are over-represented among the diaspora, is an important reason for this, although there is an active campaign to allow temporary migrant workers to participate in elections.

South Africa

South African emigrants were able to vote for the first time in the general election in April 2009. An estimated 16,000 emigrants, and 23 million South African residents had registered to vote, so the perceived anti-ANC bias of emigrants was never likely to affect the overall result.

Cook Islands

From 1981, the 6,000 Cook Islanders overseas eligible to vote could directly elect a member of parliament, but their votes carried less weight than those of the 18,000 Cook Islands residents, who elected the remaining 24 MPs. As few overseas Cook Islanders actually voted, the system was abandoned in 2003.

DUAL NATIONALITY

An increasingly mobile global population is creating a large number of people with dual nationality – and a range of responses from governments.

The citizenship held by any individual may be that of the country where they were born (the legal principle of *jus soli*) or that of their parents' nationality *(jus sanguinis)*. Citizenship at birth is usually influenced by both. If the nationality of each parent is different and both parents are granted the right to pass on their nationality, or if the state in which a child is born is different from the state of citizenship of his or her parents, the child will potentially have dual nationality. Individuals may also acquire citizenship through marriage, or following a long period of residency. If they do not renounce their previous citizenship, they also become dual citizens.

Countries have tried to prevent dual citizenship. In 1850, treaties were agreed that eliminated the possibility of dual nationality between the USA and certain European states. In 1930, the League of Nations opposed dual nationality in its Convention on Certain Questions Relating to the Conflict of Nationality Laws, and as late as 1963 the

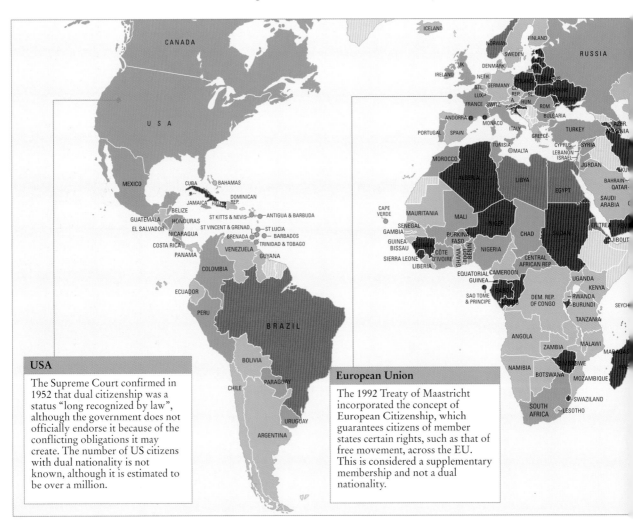

USA

The Supreme Court confirmed in 1952 that dual citizenship was a status "long recognized by law", although the government does not officially endorse it because of the conflicting obligations it may create. The number of US citizens with dual nationality is not known, although it is estimated to be over a million.

European Union

The 1992 Treaty of Maastricht incorporated the concept of European Citizenship, which guarantees citizens of member states certain rights, such as that of free movement, across the EU. This is considered a supplementary membership and not a dual nationality.

Council of Europe drew up the Convention on the Reduction of Cases of Multiple Nationality. Governments were keen to avoid situations in which individuals had obligations to more than one nation-state, particularly in cases of war. For a country of immigrants, such as the USA, this was particularly important.

Yet governments have been powerless to halt the increase in dual nationality. As migration has become more common, and the right of women to pass on their nationality to their children has become increasingly widely recognized, occurrence of dual or even multiple citizenship is unavoidable. Most countries now recognize at least some circumstances under which dual nationality will occur. In countries that revoke the citizenship of those acquiring another nationality it is difficult to work out how widespread the practice of dual nationality actually is.

ATTITUDES TO DUAL NATIONALITY
2009

- recognized, though usually not endorsed
- generally not recognized, but broad exceptions (e.g. children up to age 21, marriage to foreign national)
- not recognized, but certain limited exceptions (e.g. presidential permission)
- not recognized under any circumstances
- no data

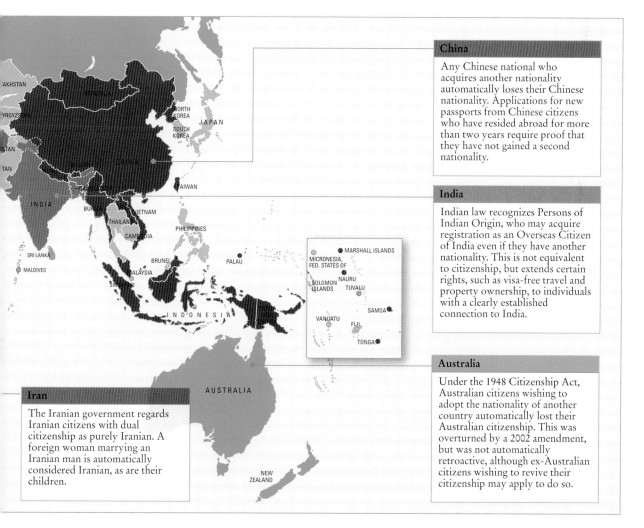

China

Any Chinese national who acquires another nationality automatically loses their Chinese nationality. Applications for new passports from Chinese citizens who have resided abroad for more than two years require proof that they have not gained a second nationality.

India

Indian law recognizes Persons of Indian Origin, who may acquire registration as an Overseas Citizen of India even if they have another nationality. This is not equivalent to citizenship, but extends certain rights, such as visa-free travel and property ownership, to individuals with a clearly established connection to India.

Australia

Under the 1948 Citizenship Act, Australian citizens wishing to adopt the nationality of another country automatically lost their Australian citizenship. This was overturned by a 2002 amendment, but was not automatically retroactive, although ex-Australian citizens wishing to revive their citizenship may apply to do so.

Iran

The Iranian government regards Iranian citizens with dual citizenship as purely Iranian. A foreign woman marrying an Iranian man is automatically considered Iranian, as are their children.

REMITTANCES & DEVELOPMENT

Remittances sent by migrant workers can make a substantial contribution to the economic and social development of their home country.

Debate about the relationship between migration and development has long focused on the role played by poverty and a lack of development in creating the conditions that force people to migrate. Yet there is growing awareness that the relationship may also work in the opposite direction – that migration may represent an important strategy for individuals and households to promote development and escape poverty. This is seen most clearly in the growing volume of international remittances worldwide, which has significant potential consequences for developing countries. Estimates suggest that the global flow of migrant workers' remittances to developing countries was over $250 billion in 2007, with this including only those remittances sent through official channels. Since, in many countries of emigration, a substantial proportion of remittances is sent through informal channels, the total volume of remittances is certainly considerably higher.

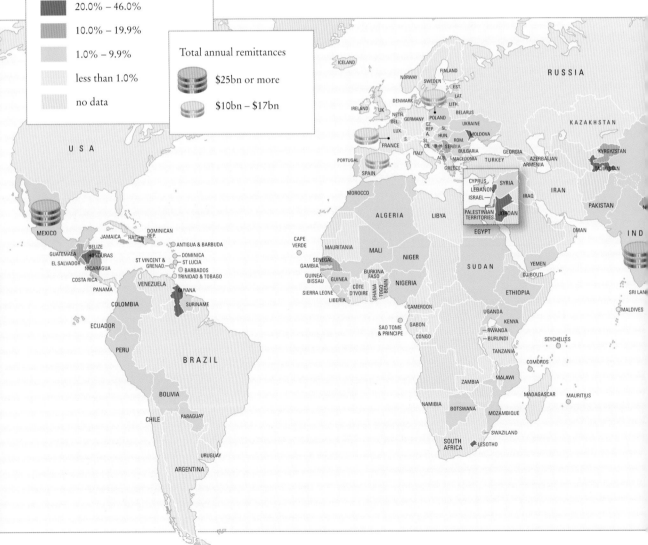

REMITTANCES
As percentage of recipient country GDP
2007

- 20.0% – 46.0%
- 10.0% – 19.9%
- 1.0% – 9.9%
- less than 1.0%
- no data

Total annual remittances

- $25bn or more
- $10bn – $17bn

While the countries with the largest volume of remittances are, unsurprisingly, among the most populous, when remittances are calculated as a percentage of a country's economy, a different picture emerges. Tajikistan, with nearly half of its GDP coming from remittances, is most dependent on this source of income, followed by Moldova and Lesotho.

Given the size of estimated remittances by migrants to poor countries, it is not surprising that these flows are of interest to development policy-makers. The World Bank argues that workers' remittances are a particularly stable source of external development finance for developing countries, reacting in a less volatile way to economic booms and downturns, and likely to rise over the medium term.

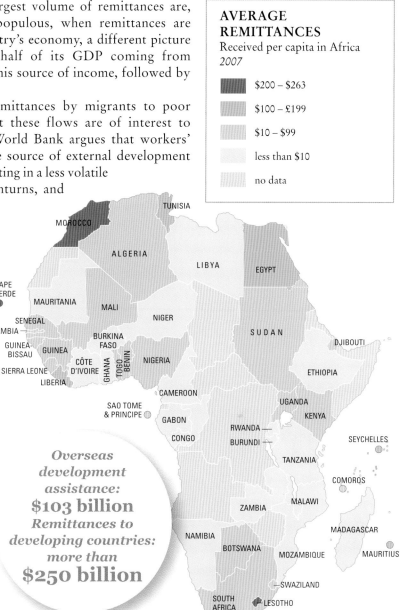

AVERAGE REMITTANCES
Received per capita in Africa
2007

- $200 – $263
- $100 – £199
- $10 – $99
- less than $10
- no data

Overseas development assistance:
$103 billion
Remittances to developing countries: more than
$250 billion

Recent research in Ghana has shown how remittances reduce the level, depth, and severity of poverty, whilst work in Pakistan has shown how migrant remittances are invested in the education of girls, with significant effects on school enrolment and improvement in grades. However, given that it is often not the poorest in a community who are able to migrate internationally, there are some concerns that migration increases levels of inequality in poorer sending communities.

MIGRATION POLICY

Despite national and international political debates about migration, government policies remain surprisingly varied.

Although the global economic crises of the 1970s and 1980s produced political pressure for governments of rich countries to clamp down on immigration in order to protect jobs for their citizens, in practice, their immigration policies show significant variation.

In the immediate aftermath of the 1970s oil crisis, a number of European countries – including France and Germany – did seek to limit further immigration from the south, and often tried to encourage immigrants to return to their country of origin. However, improved economic conditions in the 1990s led some European countries to look more favourably on immigration, and in 2005 only seven of the then-25 EU member states were trying to lower immigration, whilst six more had policies geared towards recruiting immigrants.

The emphasis among the traditional countries of immigration is mostly on recruiting highly skilled migrants. Such policies have also spread to more recent destinations for migrants, such as Russia,

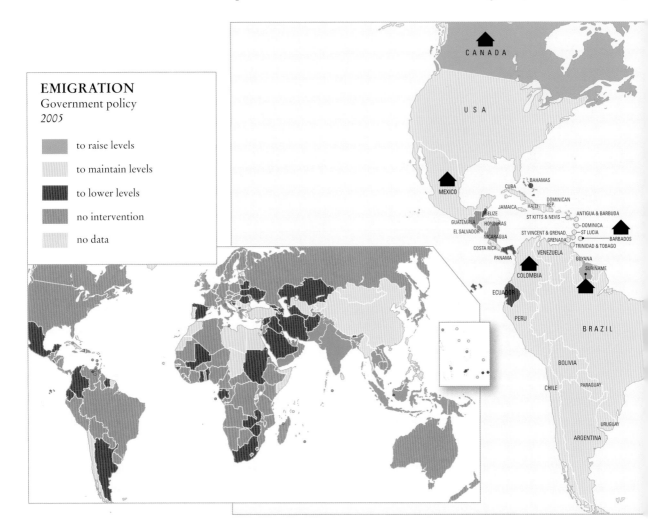

EMIGRATION
Government policy
2005

- to raise levels
- to maintain levels
- to lower levels
- no intervention
- no data

Singapore and Japan. This reflects an understanding that there is a growing global competition for skilled people in sectors such as health, information technology and other professional services.

Some poorer countries have also sought to attract skilled migrants, but many more are, perhaps surprisingly, focused on reducing immigration. For example, amongst poor countries in Asia, only Laos is seeking to recruit skilled immigrants, whilst in Africa, Zambia is the sole country with a pro-immigration policy. In Africa, in particular, this seems to reflect a general suspicion of migration, and not just of immigration.

Despite much recent talk of policies on "migration and development", relatively few countries say they are seeking to promote emigration, and all are in Asia. And whilst a small number of countries are considering trying to emulate the practice in the Philippines of training workers for export, this remains highly exceptional.

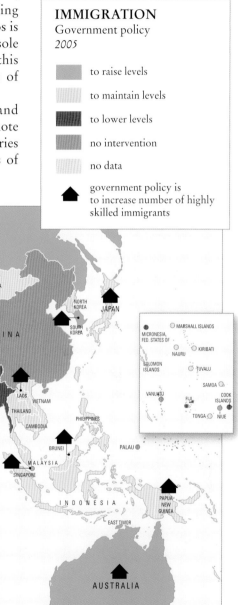

IMMIGRATION
Government policy
2005

to raise levels

to maintain levels

to lower levels

no intervention

no data

government policy is
to increase number of highly
skilled immigrants

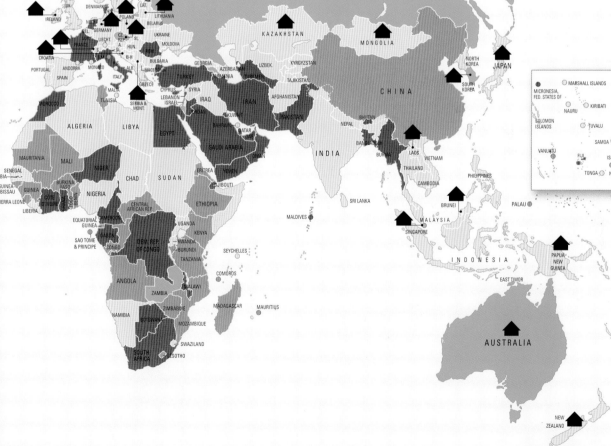

Part Four

DATA & SOURCES

The basic data used for the study of population migration are often weak and subject to error. Only for the most advanced countries of the world do we have reasonably accurate information on population flows and, even here, very few countries provide information on the number of people leaving. Emigration and return migration are particularly problematic areas for robust data.

For the study of international migration, the basic data are provided by the United Nations and refer to the stock of the foreign-born, or those living in a country other than the one in which they were born. Where place of birth is not available, citizenship is substituted, although this is not ideal for the study of migration. These national stock data are represented on pages 40–41, and listed in the following table. A more complex set of data, disaggregated to provide global estimates of origin–destination, is also available on the Global Migrant Origin Database.

The UNHCR provides detailed annual statistics on refugees at the global level which are presented here. Data on IDPs are much more difficult to collect. The most authoritative source is the Internal Displacement Monitoring Centre (IDMC), which collates information from a variety of surveys and media sources in order to arrive at "best estimates" which have been used here.

Data on internal migration are often based on place of birth, although place of residence at a previous point in time provides more recent information on flows. Because of the different definitions of "a migrant" and the different sizes of migration-defining spatial units, cross-country comparisons of internal migration are difficult.

The basic population data are supplemented by information from large-scale surveys such as labour-force surveys, demographic and health surveys, living standards measurement surveys, and, in a small number of cases, national migration surveys. A multitude of small-scale surveys provide insight on particular themes. Specialized databases on students, skilled migrants and refugees are also available from international organizations or specialized agencies of the United Nations. Remittance data are generally extracted from national accounts statistics, although these can also be supplemented by specialized surveys.

Would-be migrants to Europe being transported across the Algerian desert. The very nature of irregular migration makes it hard to quantify accurately.

Economics & Movement

	Total population	GDP per capita purchasing power parity $	Remittances as % of GDP	Migrants		Net migration Average annual rate per 1,000 population
	millions 2008	2008	2007	1,000s 2010	as % of population 2010	2005–10
Afghanistan	27.2	–	–	91	0.30%	7.5
Albania	3.1	7,715	13.6%	89	2.80%	−4.8
Algeria	34.4	8,033	1.6%	242	0.70%	−0.8
Angola	18.0	5,899	–	65	0.30%	0.9
Antigua & Barbuda	0.1	21,323	2.0%	21	23.60%	–
Argentina	39.9	14,333	0.2%	1,449	3.60%	0.2
Armenia	3.1	6,070	9.2%	324	10.50%	−4.9
Australia	21.4	35,677	0.5%	4,711	21.90%	4.8
Austria	8.3	38,152	0.8%	1,310	15.60%	3.9
Azerbaijan	8.7	8,765	4.1%	264	3.00%	−1.2
Bahamas	0.3	–	–	33	9.70%	1.2
Bahrain	0.8	–	–	315	39.10%	5.2
Bangladesh	160.0	1,334	9.6%	1,085	0.70%	−0.7
Barbados	0.3	–	4.1%	28	10.90%	−1.0
Belarus	9.7	12,261	0.8%	1,090	11.40%	–
Belgium	10.7	34,493	1.9%	975	9.10%	3.8
Belize	0.3	6,941	5.9%	47	15.00%	−0.7
Benin	8.7	1,468	4.1%	232	2.50%	1.2
Bhutan	0.7	4,755	–	40	5.70%	2.9
Bolivia	9.7	4,278	7.1%	146	1.50%	−2.1
Bosnia & Herzegovina	3.8	8,390	17.8%	28	0.70%	−0.5
Botswana	1.9	13,392	1.1%	115	5.80%	1.6
Brazil	192.0	10,296	0.3%	688	0.40%	−0.2
Brunei	0.4	–	–	148	36.40%	1.8
Bulgaria	7.6	12,393	5.4%	107	1.40%	−1.3
Burkina Faso	15.2	1,161	0.7%	1,043	6.40%	−0.9
Burma	49.2	–	0.6%	89	0.20%	−2.0
Burundi	8.1	383	0.0%	61	0.70%	8.1
Cambodia	14.7	1,905	4.2%	336	2.20%	−0.1
Cameroon	18.9	2,215	0.8%	197	1.00%	−0.2
Canada	33.3	36,444	–	7,202	21.30%	6.3
Cape Verde	0.5	3,504	9.7%	12	2.40%	−5.1
Central African Republic	4.4	736	–	80	1.80%	0.2
Chad	11.1	1,455	–	388	3.40%	−1.4
Chile	16.8	14,465	0.0%	320	1.90%	0.4
China	1,325.6	5,962	1.0%	686	0.10%	−0.3
Colombia	44.5	8,885	2.2%	110	0.20%	−0.5
Comoros	0.6	1,169	2.7%	14	2.00%	−3.1
Congo	3.6	3,946	0.2%	143	3.80%	−2.8
Congo, Dem. Rep.	64.2	321	–	445	0.70%	−0.3
Cook Islands	0.0	–	–	3	14.10%	−3.2
Costa Rica	4.5	11,241	2.4%	489	10.50%	1.3
Côte d'Ivoire	20.6	1,651	0.9%	2,407	11.20%	−1.4
Croatia	4.4	19,084	2.7%	700	15.90%	0.5
Cuba	11.2	–	–	15	0.10%	−3.5
Cyprus	0.9	–	0.8%	154	17.50%	5.8
Czech Republic	10.4	24,712	0.8%	453	4.40%	4.4
Denmark	5.5	36,607	0.3%	484	8.80%	1.1

Refugees and others by country of origin end 2008			Refugees and others by country of asylum end 2008			
Refugees	Returned refugees	Total population of concern	Refugees	Refugees per 1,000 population	IDPs	
2,833,128	278,489	3,371,919	37	0	at least 235,000	Afghanistan
15,006	–	16,828	65	0	–	Albania
9,060	–	10,596	94,093	3	undetermined	Algeria
171,393	13,052	185,186	12,710	1	undetermined	Angola
26	–	52	–	–	–	Antigua & Barbuda
1,047	1	1,191	2,845	0	–	Argentina
16,336	1	20,105	3,953	1	8,400	Armenia
43	–	53	20,919	1	–	Australia
14	–	16	37,557	4	–	Austria
16,319	–	621,914	2,061	0	573,000 – 603,000	Azerbaijan
15	–	40	–	0	–	Bahamas
80	–	93	48	0	–	Bahrain
10,098	–	16,809	28,389	0	60,000 – 500,000	Bangladesh
34	–	83	–	–	–	Barbados
5,384	–	8,883	609	0	–	Belarus
61	–	89	17,026	2	–	Belgium
20	–	39	277	1	–	Belize
318	–	505	6,933	1	–	Benin
104,965	–	106,056	–	–	–	Bhutan
454	–	615	664	0	–	Bolivia
74,366	971	252,236	7,257	2	125,000	Bosnia & Herzegovina
26	–	179	3,019	2	–	Botswana
1,404	–	1,773	3,852	0	–	Brazil
1	–	1	–	–	–	Brunei
3,040	–	3,340	5,129	1	–	Bulgaria
725	–	1,042	557	0	–	Burkina Faso
184,413	–	274,041	–	0	at least 451,000	Burma
281,592	95,389	483,626	21,093	3	100,000	Burundi
17,253	–	17,471	164	0	–	Cambodia
13,870	–	16,803	81,037	4	–	Cameroon
101	–	162	173,651	5	–	Canada
30	–	37	–	0	–	Cape Verde
125,106	18	323,357	7,429	2	108,000	Central African Republic
55,105	4,415	267,222	330,510	29	180,000	Chad
994	–	1,118	1,613	0	–	Chile
175,180	–	194,805	300,967	0	–	China
373,532	31	3,426,198	170	0	2,650,000 – 4,360,000	Colombia
378	–	418	–	0	–	Comoros
19,925	105	25,069	24,779	7	up to 7,800	Congo
367,995	54,043	1,918,424	155,162	2	1,400,000	Congo, Dem. Rep.
–	–	–	–	–	–	Cook Islands
354	–	420	18,136	4	–	Costa Rica
22,227	49	737,792	24,811	1	at least 621,000	Côte d'Ivoire
97,012	1,147	129,253	1,597	0	2,600	Croatia
7,938	–	8,820	525	0	–	Cuba
10	–	12	1,465	2	up to 201,000	Cyprus
1,358	–	2,148	2,110	0	–	Czech Republic
11	–	18	23,401	4	–	Denmark

Economics & Movement

	Total population millions 2008	GDP per capita purchasing power parity $ 2008	Remittances as % of GDP 2007	Migrants 1,000s 2010	Migrants as % of population 2010	Net migration Average annual rate per 1,000 population 2005–10
Djibouti	0.8	2,140	3.4%	114	13.00%	–
Dominica	0.1	8,696	7.9%	6	8.30%	−9.0
Dominican Republic	9.8	8,217	9.3%	434	4.20%	−2.8
East Timor	1.1	801	–	14	1.20%	1.8
Ecuador	13.5	8,009	7.0%	394	2.90%	−5.2
Egypt	81.5	5,416	5.9%	245	0.30%	−0.8
El Salvador	6.1	6,794	18.2%	40	0.70%	−9.1
Equatorial Guinea	0.7	33,873	–	7	1.10%	3.1
Eritrea	5.0	632	–	16	0.30%	2.3
Estonia	1.3	20,662	2.0%	182	13.60%	–
Ethiopia	80.7	868	1.8%	548	0.60%	−0.8
Fiji	0.8	4,382	4.8%	19	2.20%	−8.3
Finland	5.3	35,427	0.3%	226	4.20%	2.1
France	62.0	34,045	0.5%	6,685	10.70%	1.6
Gabon	1.4	14,527	0.1%	284	18.90%	0.7
Gambia	1.7	1,363	7.4%	290	16.60%	1.8
Georgia	4.4	4,896	6.8%	167	4.00%	−11.5
Germany	82.1	35,613	0.3%	10,758	13.10%	1.3
Ghana	23.4	1,452	0.8%	1,852	7.60%	−0.4
Greece	11.2	29,361	0.8%	1,133	10.10%	2.7
Grenada	0.1	8,541	9.2%	13	12.10%	−9.7
Guatemala	13.7	4,760	12.6%	59	0.40%	−3.0
Guinea	9.8	1,204	3.3%	395	3.80%	−6.1
Guinea–Bissau	1.6	538	8.1%	19	1.20%	−1.6
Guyana	0.8	2,542	25.8%	12	1.50%	−10.5
Haiti	9.8	1,177	18.2%	35	0.30%	−2.9
Honduras	7.2	3,965	21.5%	24	0.30%	−2.8
Hungary	10.0	19,330	1.8%	368	3.70%	1.5
Iceland	0.3	36,775	0.2%	37	11.30%	12.8
India	1,140.0	2,972	3.3%	5,436	0.40%	−0.2
Indonesia	228.2	3,975	1.4%	123	0.10%	−0.6
Iran	72.0	11,666	0.4%	2,129	2.80%	−1.4
Iraq	28.9	–	0.6%	83	0.30%	−3.9
Ireland	4.5	44,200	0.2%	899	19.60%	9.1
Israel	7.3	27,548	0.6%	2,940	40.40%	2.4
Italy	59.9	30,756	0.2%	4,463	7.40%	5.6
Jamaica	2.7	7,705	18.8%	30	1.10%	−7.4
Japan	127.7	34,099	0.0%	2,176	1.70%	0.2
Jordan	5.9	5,283	21.7%	2,973	45.90%	8.3
Kazakhstan	15.7	11,315	0.2%	3,079	19.50%	−1.3
Kenya	38.5	1,590	6.6%	818	2.00%	−1.0
Kiribati	0.1	2,484	9.0%	2	2.00%	−2.1
Korea, North	23.9	–	–	37	0.20%	–
Korea, South	48.6	27,939	0.1%	535	1.10%	−0.1
Kuwait	2.7	–	–	2,098	68.80%	8.3
Kyrgyzstan	5.3	2,188	19.1%	223	4.00%	−2.8
Laos	6.2	2,134	0.0%	19	0.30%	−2.4
Latvia	2.3	17,100	2.0%	335	15.00%	−0.9

Refugees and others by country of origin *end 2008*			Refugees and others by country of asylum *end 2008*			
Refugees	Returned refugees	Total population of concern	Refugees	Refugees per 1,000 population	IDPs	
650	–	716	9,228	11	–	Djibouti
56	–	79	–	–	–	Dominica
318	–	588	–	0	–	Dominican Republic
7	–	15,869	1	0	30,000	East Timor
1,066	–	1,310	101,398	7	–	Ecuador
6,780	–	8,608	97,861	1	–	Egypt
5,151	–	16,311	32	0	–	El Salvador
384	1	431	–	0	–	Equatorial Guinea
186,398	92	201,094	4,862	1	undetermined	Eritrea
248	–	286	22	0	–	Estonia
63,878	167	95,552	83,583	1	200,000 – 300,000	Ethiopia
1,868	–	2,069	–	0	–	Fiji
4	–	4	6,617	1	–	Finland
101	–	159	160,017	3	–	France
129	–	162	9,001	6	–	Gabon
1,352	–	2,489	14,836	9	–	Gambia
12,598	–	413,532	996	0	252,000 – 279,000	Georgia
166	–	22,769	582,735	7	–	Germany
13,242	–	15,258	18,206	1	–	Ghana
67	–	83	2,164	0	–	Greece
312	–	378	–	–	–	Grenada
5,934	–	16,187	130	0	undetermined	Guatemala
9,495	6	11,517	21,488	2	–	Guinea
1,065	–	1,342	7,884	5	–	Guinea–Bissau
708	–	984	–	–	–	Guyana
23,066	–	35,737	3	0	–	Haiti
1,116	–	2,059	24	0	–	Honduras
1,614	–	1,908	7,750	1	–	Hungary
7	–	7	49	0	–	Iceland
19,569	–	26,445	184,543	0	at least 500,000	India
19,345	1	21,574	369	0	70,000 – 120,000	Indonesia
69,061	95	80,316	980,109	13	–	Iran
1,903,519	25,644	4,797,979	39,503	1	2,840,000	Iraq
7	–	10	9,730	2	–	Ireland
1,494	–	3,633	9,137	1	200,000	Israel
62	–	96	47,061	1	–	Italy
826	–	1,230	–	0	–	Jamaica
185	–	217	2,019	0	–	Japan
1,890	1	2,650	500,413	79	–	Jordan
4,825	–	5,411	4,352	0	–	Kazakhstan
9,688	723	762,617	320,605	8	300,000 – 600,000	Kenya
38	–	39	–	–	–	Kiribati
886	–	1,097	–	–	–	Korea, North
1,104	–	1,615	172	0	–	Korea, South
854	–	922	38,238	13	–	Kuwait
2,517	–	2,924	375	0	–	Kyrgyzstan
8,598	–	8,780	–	0	–	Laos
763	–	794	32	0	–	Latvia

ECONOMICS & MOVEMENT

	Total population	GDP per capita purchasing power parity $	Remittances as % of GDP	Migrants		Net migration Average annual rate per 1,000 population
	millions 2008	2008	2007	1,000s 2010	as % of population 2010	2005–10
Lebanon	4.1	11,570	23.7%	758	17.80%	−0.6
Lesotho	2.0	1,588	27.7%	6	0.30%	−3.5
Liberia	3.8	388	8.8%	96	2.30%	13.3
Libya	6.3	15,402	0.0%	682	10.40%	0.6
Lithuania	3.4	18,824	3.7%	129	4.00%	−6.0
Luxembourg	0.5	78,599	3.2%	173	35.20%	8.4
Macedonia	2.0	10,041	4.5%	130	6.30%	−1.0
Madagascar	19.1	1,049	0.1%	38	0.20%	−0.1
Malawi	14.3	837	0.0%	276	1.80%	−0.3
Malaysia	27.0	14,215	1.0%	2,358	8.40%	1
Maldives	0.3	5,504	0.3%	3	1.00%	–
Mali	12.7	1,128	5.0%	163	1.20%	−3.2
Malta	0.4	–	0.6%	15	3.80%	2.5
Marshall Islands	0.1	–	–	2	2.70%	−8.3
Mauritania	3.2	–	0.1%	99	2.90%	0.6
Mauritius	1.3	12,079	3.2%	43	3.30%	–
Mexico	106.4	14,495	2.7%	726	0.70%	−4.5
Micronesia, Fed. Sts.	0.1	2,830	–	3	2.40%	−16.3
Moldova	3.6	2,925	34.1%	408	11.40%	−9.4
Mongolia	2.6	3,566	4.9%	10	0.40%	−0.8
Montenegro	0.6	13,951	–	43	6.80%	−1.6
Morocco	31.2	4,388	9.0%	49	0.20%	−2.7
Mozambique	21.8	855	1.3%	450	1.90%	−0.2
Namibia	2.1	6,343	0.2%	139	6.30%	−0.1
Nauru	–	–	–	5	51.80%	−9.0
Nepal	28.6	1,112	16.8%	946	3.20%	−0.7
Netherlands	16.4	40,849	0.3%	1,753	10.50%	1.2
New Zealand	4.3	27,029	0.5%	962	22.40%	2.4
Nicaragua	5.7	2,682	12.9%	40	0.70%	−7.1
Niger	14.7	684	1.9%	202	1.30%	−0.4
Nigeria	151.3	2,082	5.6%	1,128	0.70%	−0.4
Niue	–	–	–	0	25.60%	−32.4
Norway	4.8	58,138	0.2%	485	10.00%	5.7
Oman	2.8	–	0.1%	826	28.40%	1.4
Pakistan	166.0	2,644	4.2%	4,234	2.30%	−1.6
Palau	0.0	–	–	6	28.10%	−4.9
Palestinian Territories	3.8	–	14.9%	1,924	43.60%	−0.5
Panama	3.4	12,504	0.9%	121	3.40%	0.7
Papua New Guinea	6.4	2,208	0.2%	25	0.40%	–
Paraguay	6.2	4,709	4.0%	161	2.50%	−1.3
Peru	28.8	8,507	2.0%	38	0.10%	−4.4
Philippines	90.3	3,510	11.3%	435	0.50%	−2.0
Poland	38.1	17,625	2.5%	827	2.20%	−0.6
Portugal	10.6	23,074	1.8%	919	8.60%	3.8
Puerto Rico	4.0	–	–	324	8.10%	−1.1
Qatar	1.3	–	–	1,305	86.50%	93.9
Romania	21.5	14,065	5.1%	133	0.60%	−1.9
Russia	141.8	16,139	0.4%	12,270	8.70%	0.4

Refugees and others by country of origin end 2008			Refugees and others by country of asylum end 2008			
Refugees	Returned refugees	Total population of concern	Refugees	Refugees per 1,000 population	IDPs	
12,967	–	15,258	50,419	12	90,000 – 390,000	Lebanon
8	–	25	–	0	–	Lesotho
75,213	10,806	88,413	10,224	3	undetermined	Liberia
2,084	–	2,849	6,713	1	–	Libya
490	–	550	751	0	–	Lithuania
–	–	–	3,109	6	–	Luxembourg
7,521	–	8,605	1,672	1	770	Macedonia
277	–	294	–	0	–	Madagascar
106	–	8,316	4,175	0	–	Malawi
608	–	62,063	36,671	1	–	Malaysia
16	–	17	–	–	–	Maldives
1,758	–	2,508	9,578	1	–	Mali
9	–	9	4,331	11	–	Malta
–	–	–	–	–	–	Marshall Islands
45,601	7,036	53,421	27,041	8	–	Mauritania
24	–	49	–	0	–	Mauritius
6,162	–	23,605	1,055	0	5,500 – 21,000	Mexico
–	–	–	1	0	–	Micronesia, Fed. Sts.
5,555	–	6,443	148	0	–	Moldova
1,333	–	3,403	11	0	–	Mongolia
1,283	–	1,464	24,741	40	–	Montenegro
3,533	–	4,067	766	0	–	Morocco
208	–	890	3,163	0	–	Mozambique
985	20	1,033	6,799	3	–	Namibia
3	–	4	–	–	–	Nauru
4,189	1	6,361	124,832	4	50,000 – 70,000	Nepal
46	–	74	77,600	5	–	Netherlands
10	–	18	2,716	1	–	New Zealand
1,537	–	2,005	147	0	–	Nicaragua
796	–	1,067	320	0	–	Niger
14,169	2	24,645	10,124	0	undetermined	Nigeria
–	–	–	–	–	–	Niue
4	–	5	36,101	8	–	Norway
56	–	60	7	0	–	Oman
32,403	5	194,471	1,780,935	10	at least 480,000	Pakistan
1	–	1	–	–	–	Palau
340,016	4	342,681	–	0	116,000	Palestinian Territories
111	–	147	16,913	5	–	Panama
46	–	65	10,006	1	–	Papua New Guinea
101	–	133	75	0	–	Paraguay
7,339	1	9,843	1,075	0	150,000	Peru
1,354	–	2,351	104	0	at least 308,000	Philippines
2,391	–	2,618	12,774	0	–	Poland
36	–	71	403	0	–	Portugal
–	–	–	–	–	–	Puerto Rico
71	–	74	13	0	–	Qatar
4,756	–	5,148	1,596	0	–	Romania
103,061	70	211,447	3,479	0	82,000 – 98,000	Russia

ECONOMICS & MOVEMENT

	Total population millions 2008	GDP per capita purchasing power parity $ 2008	Remittances as % of GDP 2007	Migrants		Net migration Average annual rate per 1,000 population 2005–10
				1,000s 2010	as % of population 2010	
Rwanda	9.7	1,022	1.5%	465	4.50%	0.3
St. Kitts & Nevis	0.1	16,160	7.1%	5	9.60%	–
St. Lucia	0.2	9,907	3.2%	10	5.90%	–1.2
St. Vincent & Grenadines	0.1	9,155	5.5%	9	7.90%	–9.2
Samoa	0.2	4,485	22.8%	9	5.00%	–18.4
São Tomé & Principe	0.2	1,738	1.4%	5	3.20%	–8.8
Saudi Arabia	24.6	23,920	–	7,289	27.80%	1.2
Senegal	12.2	1,772	10.7%	210	1.60%	–1.7
Serbia	7.4	11,456	13.9%	525	5.30%	–
Seychelles	0.1	21,530	1.5%	11	12.80%	–4.8
Sierra Leone	5.6	766	8.9%	107	1.80%	2.2
Singapore	4.8	49,284	–	1,967	40.70%	22
Slovakia	5.4	22,081	2.0%	131	2.40%	0.7
Slovenia	2.0	27,605	0.6%	164	8.10%	2.2
Solomon Islands	0.5	2,610	5.3%	7	1.30%	–
Somalia	9.0	–	–	23	0.20%	–5.6
South Africa	48.7	10,109	0.3%	1,863	3.70%	2.8
Spain	45.6	31,954	0.7%	6,378	14.10%	7.9
Sri Lanka	20.2	4,560	7.8%	340	1.70%	–3.0
Sudan	41.3	2,153	3.8%	753	1.70%	0.7
Suriname	0.5	7,506	6.2%	39	7.50%	–2.0
Swaziland	1.2	4,928	3.5%	40	3.40%	–1.0
Sweden	9.2	37,383	0.2%	1,306	14.10%	3.3
Switzerland	7.6	42,536	0.5%	1,763	23.20%	2.7
Syria	21.2	4,440	2.2%	2,206	9.80%	7.7
Tajikistan	6.8	1,906	45.5%	284	4.00%	–5.9
Tanzania	42.5	1,263	0.1%	659	1.50%	–1.4
Thailand	67.4	7,703	0.7%	1,157	1.70%	0.9
Togo	6.5	829	9.2%	185	2.70%	–0.2
Tonga	0.1	3,824	39.4%	1	0.80%	–17.5
Trinidad & Tobago	1.3	24,748	0.5%	34	2.60%	–3.0
Tunisia	10.3	7,996	4.9%	34	0.30%	–0.4
Turkey	73.9	13,920	0.2%	1,411	1.90%	–0.1
Turkmenistan	5.0	6,641	–	208	4.00%	–1.0
Tuvalu	–	–	–	0	1.50%	–10.1
Uganda	31.7	1,165	3.8%	647	1.90%	–0.9
Ukraine	46.3	7,271	3.2%	5,258	11.60%	–0.3
United Arab Emirates	4.5	–	–	3,293	70.00%	15.6
United Kingdom	61.4	35,445	0.3%	6,452	10.40%	3.1
United States	304.1	46,716	0.0%	42,813	13.50%	3.3
Uruguay	3.3	12,734	0.4%	80	2.40%	–3.0
Uzbekistan	27.3	2,656	–	1,176	4.20%	–3.0
Vanuatu	0.2	3,978	1.2%	1	0.30%	–
Venezuela	27.9	12,804	0.1%	1,007	3.50%	0.3
Vietnam	86.2	2,785	8.0%	69	0.10%	–0.5
Yemen	23.1	2,400	5.9%	518	2.10%	–1.2
Zambia	12.6	1,356	0.5%	233	1.80%	–1.4
Zimbabwe	12.5	–	–	372	2.90%	

Refugees and others by country of origin end 2008			Refugees and others by country of asylum end 2008			
Refugees	Returned refugees	Total population of concern	Refugees	Refugees per 1,000 population	IDPs	
72,530	11,790	90,428	55,062	6	undetermined	Rwanda
4	–	12	–	–	–	St. Kitts & Nevis
288	–	624	–	0	–	St. Lucia
750	–	1,494	–	–	–	St. Vincent & Grenadines
4	–	4	–	–	–	Samoa
35	–	35	–	0	–	São Tomé & Principe
712	–	751	240,572	9	–	Saudi Arabia
16,006	2	16,827	33,193	3	10,000 – 70,000	Senegal
185,935	858	427,873	96,739	10	226,000	Serbia
53	–	69	–	–	–	Seychelles
32,536	321	35,480	7,826	1	–	Sierra Leone
109	–	125	10	0	–	Singapore
331	–	463	317	0	–	Slovakia
52	–	64	268	0	–	Slovenia
52	–	52	–	–	–	Solomon Islands
561,154	1,476	1,860,373	1,842	0	1,300,000	Somalia
453	–	604	43,546	1	–	South Africa
27	–	50	4,661	0	–	Spain
137,752	1,739	672,148	269	0	485,000	Sri Lanka
419,248	90,087	1,749,536	181,605	4	4,900,000	Sudan
50	–	63	1	0	–	Suriname
32	–	131	775	1	–	Swaziland
15	–	33	77,038	8	–	Sweden
32	–	38	46,132	6	–	Switzerland
15,211	8	21,208	1,105,698	50	433,000	Syria
544	–	694	1,799	0	–	Tajikistan
1,270	–	4,171	321,909	7	–	Tanzania
1,815	–	2,229	112,932	2	–	Thailand
16,750	4,798	22,679	9,377	1	undetermined	Togo
7	–	33	–	–	–	Tonga
231	–	470	33	0	–	Trinidad & Tobago
2,349	–	2,717	94	0	–	Tunisia
214,378	1	223,223	11,103	0	954,000 – 1,201,000	Turkey
736	1	852	79	0	undetermined	Turkmenistan
2	–	2	–	–	–	Tuvalu
7,548	104	1,466,792	162,132	5	869,000	Uganda
28,424	–	30,323	7,201	0	–	Ukraine
256	–	267	209	0	–	United Arab Emirates
185	–	213	292,097	5	–	United Kingdom
2,137	–	3,892	279,548	1	–	United States
199	–	250	145	0	–	Uruguay
6,308	5	8,153	821	0	3,400	Uzbekistan
–	–	–	3	0	–	Vanuatu
5,807	–	7,333	201,161	7	–	Venezuela
328,183	315	330,210	2,357	0	–	Vietnam
1,777	–	102,250	140,169	6	20,000 – 23,000	Yemen
195	–	690	83,485	6	–	Zambia
16,841	3	51,639	3,468	0	570,000 – 1,000,000	Zimbabwe

MIGRATION POLICY

	Government policy			Voting status of people living abroad in relation to elections in country of origin 2009	
	on level of immigration 2005	on highly skilled immigrants 2005	on emigration 2005		
Afghanistan	maintain	–	lower	may vote abroad	
Albania	maintain	maintain	maintain	must return to vote	
Algeria	maintain	–	no intervention	may vote abroad	
Angola	no intervention	–	no intervention	may vote abroad*	
Antigua & Barbuda	maintain	maintain	no intervention	cannot vote	
Argentina	maintain	maintain	lower	may vote abroad	
Armenia	raise	maintain	lower	cannot vote	
Australia	raise	raise	no intervention	may vote abroad	
Austria	maintain	maintain	no intervention	may vote abroad	
Azerbaijan	maintain	–	lower	may vote abroad	
Bahamas	lower	maintain	no intervention	must return to vote	
Bahrain	maintain	–	no intervention	may vote abroad	
Bangladesh	lower	–	raise	may vote abroad	
Barbados	maintain	raise	no intervention	cannot vote	
Belarus	maintain	maintain	lower	may vote abroad	
Belgium	maintain	maintain	no intervention	may vote abroad	
Belize	lower	maintain	no intervention	cannot vote	
Benin	no intervention	no intervention	lower	may vote abroad	
Bhutan	lower	lower	lower	no elections	
Bolivia	maintain	maintain	no intervention	may vote abroad	
Bosnia & Herzegovina	maintain	–	lower	may vote abroad	
Botswana	lower	lower	no intervention	may vote abroad	
Brazil	maintain	maintain	no intervention	may vote abroad	
Brunei	maintain	raise	no intervention	no elections	
Bulgaria	maintain	maintain	maintain	may vote abroad	
Burkina Faso	no intervention	no intervention	no intervention	cannot vote	
Burma	lower	maintain	maintain	cannot vote	
Burundi	no intervention	–	no intervention	may vote abroad	
Cambodia	maintain	maintain	no intervention	may vote abroad	
Cameroon	lower	–	no intervention	cannot vote	
Canada	raise	raise	no intervention	may vote abroad	
Cape Verde	no intervention	no intervention	maintain	may vote abroad*	
Central African Republic	no intervention	–	no intervention	may vote abroad	
Chad	maintain	–	maintain	may vote abroad	
Chile	maintain	maintain	maintain	must return to vote	
China	no intervention	maintain	maintain	must return to vote	
Colombia	maintain	raise	lower	may vote abroad*	
Comoros	no intervention	–	no intervention	must return to vote	
Congo	no intervention	–	no intervention	must return to vote	
Congo, Dem. Rep.	lower	–	no intervention	may vote abroad	
Cook Islands	lower	no intervention	lower	must return to vote	
Costa Rica	maintain	–	no intervention	must return to vote	
Côte d'Ivoire	lower	maintain	no intervention	may vote abroad	
Croatia	maintain	raise	lower	may vote abroad*	
Cuba	maintain	maintain	maintain	no elections	
Cyprus	lower	maintain	maintain	must return to vote	
Czech Republic	raise	raise	no intervention	may vote abroad	
Denmark	lower	raise	no intervention	cannot vote	

* may vote in legislative elections for special representative for people living outside countr

United Nations instruments Date of ratification as of *July 2009*				
1951 Refugee Convention	1967 Refugee Protocol	1990 Migrant Workers Convention	2000 Human Trafficking Protocol	
2005	2005	–	–	Afghanistan
1992	1992	2007	2002	Albania
1963	1967	2005	2004	Algeria
1981	1981	–	–	Angola
1995	1995	–	–	Antigua & Barbuda
1961	1967	2007	2002	Argentina
1993	1993	–	2003	Armenia
1954	1973	–	2005	Australia
1954	1973	–	2005	Austria
1993	1993	1999	2003	Azerbaijan
1993	1993	–	2008	Bahamas
–	–	–	2004	Bahrain
–	–	–	–	Bangladesh
–	–	–	–	Barbados
2001	2001	–	2003	Belarus
1953	1969	–	2004	Belgium
1990	1990	2001	2003	Belize
1962	1970	–	2004	Benin
–	–	–	–	Bhutan
1982	1982	2000	2006	Bolivia
1993	1993	1996	2002	Bosnia & Herzegovina
1969	1969	–	2002	Botswana
1960	1972	–	2004	Brazil
–	–	–	–	Brunei
1993	1993	–	2001	Bulgaria
1980	1980	2003	2002	Burkina Faso
–	–	–	2004	Burma
1963	1971	–	–	Burundi
1992	1992	–	2007	Cambodia
1961	1967	–	2006	Cameroon
1969	1969	–	2002	Canada
–	1987	1997	2004	Cape Verde
1962	1967	–	2006	Central African Republic
1981	1981	–	–	Chad
1972	1972	2005	2004	Chile
1982	1982	–	–	China
1961	1980	1995	2004	Colombia
–	–	–	–	Comoros
1962	1970	–	–	Congo
1965	1975	–	2005	Congo, Dem. Rep.
-	-	-	-	Cook Islands
1978	1978	–	2003	Costa Rica
1961	1970	–	–	Côte d'Ivoire
1992	1992	–	2003	Croatia
–	–	–	–	Cuba
1963	1968	–	2003	Cyprus
1993	1993	–	–	Czech Republic
1952	1968	–	2003	Denmark

MIGRATION POLICY

	Government policy			Voting status of people living abroad in relation to elections in country of origin 2009
	on level of immigration 2005	on highly skilled immigrants 2005	on emigration 2005	
Djibouti	lower	–	no intervention	may vote abroad
Dominica	maintain	maintain	no intervention	cannot vote
Dominican Republic	maintain	–	no intervention	may vote abroad
East Timor	maintain	maintain	no intervention	no data
Ecuador	lower	maintain	lower	may vote abroad
Egypt	lower	maintain	maintain	cannot vote
El Salvador	no intervention	maintain	lower	cannot vote
Equatorial Guinea	no intervention	–	lower	may vote abroad
Eritrea	no intervention	–	no intervention	may vote abroad
Estonia	lower	maintain	maintain	no data
Ethiopia	no intervention	no intervention	no intervention	must return to vote
Fiji	lower	–	lower	may vote abroad
Finland	maintain	maintain	no intervention	may vote abroad
France	lower	raise	no intervention	may vote abroad*
Gabon	lower	–	lower	may vote abroad
Gambia	lower	no intervention	no intervention	must return to vote
Georgia	maintain	maintain	lower	may vote abroad
Germany	maintain	raise	no intervention	may vote abroad
Ghana	lower	no intervention	lower	may vote abroad
Greece	maintain	maintain	no intervention	may vote abroad
Grenada	maintain	maintain	lower	cannot vote
Guatemala	no intervention	maintain	no intervention	cannot vote
Guinea	no intervention	no intervention	no intervention	may vote abroad
Guinea-Bissau	no intervention	–	lower	may vote abroad*
Guyana	maintain	maintain	no intervention	may vote abroad
Haiti	maintain	–	lower	may vote abroad*
Honduras	maintain	maintain	no intervention	may vote abroad
Hungary	maintain	–	no intervention	may vote abroad
Iceland	no intervention	no intervention	no intervention	may vote abroad
India	maintain	maintain	raise	cannot vote
Indonesia	maintain	maintain	raise	may vote abroad
Iran	lower	maintain	lower	may vote abroad
Iraq	maintain	maintain	lower	may vote abroad
Ireland	maintain	raise	no intervention	cannot vote
Israel	raise	maintain	lower	must return to vote
Italy	lower	no intervention	no intervention	may vote abroad*
Jamaica	maintain	maintain	no intervention	cannot vote
Japan	maintain	raise	no intervention	may vote abroad
Jordan	lower	lower	raise	cannot vote
Kazakhstan	maintain	raise	lower	may vote abroad
Kenya	no intervention	no intervention	no intervention	must return to vote
Kiribati	maintain	–	maintain	cannot vote
Korea, North	maintain	maintain	maintain	no data
Korea, South	raise	raise	no intervention	no elections
Kuwait	lower	maintain	no intervention	cannot vote
Kyrgyzstan	maintain	maintain	maintain	may vote abroad
Laos	maintain	raise	no intervention	cannot vote
Latvia	maintain	maintain	no intervention	may vote abroad

* may vote in legislative elections for special representative for people living outside country

United Nations instruments Date of ratification as of *July 2009*				
1951 Refugee Convention	1967 Refugee Protocol	1990 Migrant Workers Convention	2000 Human Trafficking Protocol	
1977	1977	–	2005	Djibouti
1994	1994	–	–	Dominica
1978	1978	–	2008	Dominican Republic
2003	2003	2004	–	East Timor
1955	1969	2002	2002	Ecuador
1981	1981	1993	2004	Egypt
1983	1983	2003	2004	El Salvador
1986	1986	–	2003	Equatorial Guinea
–	–	–	–	Eritrea
1997	1997	–	2004	Estonia
1969	1969	–	–	Ethiopia
1972	1972	–	–	Fiji
1968	1968	–	2006	Finland
1954	1971	–	2002	France
1964	1973	–	–	Gabon
1966	1967	–	2003	Gambia
1999	1999	–	2006	Georgia
1953	1969	–	2006	Germany
1963	1968	2000	–	Ghana
1960	1968	–	–	Greece
–	–	–	2004	Grenada
1983	1983	2003	2004	Guatemala
1965	1968	2000	2004	Guinea
1976	1976	–	2007	Guinea-Bissau
–	–	–	2004	Guyana
1984	1984	–	–	Haiti
1992	1992	2005	2008	Honduras
1989	1989	–	2006	Hungary
1955	1968	–	–	Iceland
–	–	–	–	India
–	–	–	–	Indonesia
1976	1976	–	–	Iran
–	–	–	2009	Iraq
1956	1968	–	–	Ireland
1954	1968	–	2008	Israel
1954	1972	–	2006	Italy
1964	1980	2008	2003	Jamaica
1981	1982	–	–	Japan
–	–	–	2009	Jordan
1999	1999	–	2008	Kazakhstan
1966	1981	–	2005	Kenya
–	–	–	2005	Kiribati
–	–	–	–	Korea, North
1992	1992	–	–	Korea, South
–	–	–	2006	Kuwait
1996	1996	2003	2003	Kyrgyzstan
–	–	–	2003	Laos
1997	1997	–	2004	Latvia

MIGRATION POLICY

	Government policy			Voting status of people living abroad in relation to elections in country of origin 2009
	on level of immigration 2005	on highly skilled immigrants 2005	on emigration 2005	
Lebanon	lower	no intervention	lower	must return to vote
Lesotho	no intervention	–	no intervention	may vote abroad
Liberia	maintain	–	no intervention	must return to vote
Libya	maintain	–	maintain	no elections
Lithuania	maintain	raise	no intervention	may vote abroad
Luxembourg	maintain	–	no intervention	may vote abroad
Macedonia	maintain	–	lower	cannot vote
Madagascar	no intervention	–	no intervention	cannot vote
Malawi	lower	–	no intervention	must return to vote
Malaysia	maintain	maintain	no intervention	may vote abroad
Maldives	lower	–	no intervention	cannot vote
Mali	no intervention	–	lower	may vote abroad
Malta	maintain	maintain	no intervention	cannot vote
Marshall Islands	maintain	–	maintain	may vote abroad
Mauritania	no intervention	–	no intervention	cannot vote
Mauritius	no intervention	no intervention	no intervention	cannot vote
Mexico	maintain	raise	lower	may vote abroad
Micronesia, Fed. Sts.	lower	maintain	no intervention	may vote abroad
Moldova	maintain	–	no intervention	may vote abroad
Mongolia	maintain	raise	maintain	must return to vote
Montenegro	–	–	–	no elections
Morocco	lower	maintain	maintain	may vote abroad*
Mozambique	no intervention	–	no intervention	may vote abroad*
Namibia	maintain	maintain	no intervention	may vote abroad
Nauru	maintain	–	maintain	may vote abroad
Nepal	maintain	maintain	raise	cannot vote
Netherlands	lower	raise	no intervention	may vote abroad
New Zealand	maintain	raise	no intervention	may vote abroad
Nicaragua	no intervention	no intervention	no intervention	must return to vote
Niger	lower	–	no intervention	cannot vote
Nigeria	maintain	–	no intervention	cannot vote
Niue	raise	–	lower	–
Norway	maintain	raise	no intervention	may vote abroad
Oman	lower	maintain	no intervention	no data
Pakistan	lower	maintain	raise	cannot vote
Palau	no intervention	–	lower	may vote abroad
Palestinian Territories	–	–	–	no data
Panama	lower	–	no intervention	may vote abroad
Papua New Guinea	maintain	raise	no intervention	cannot vote
Paraguay	maintain	maintain	no intervention	cannot vote
Peru	maintain	maintain	no intervention	may vote abroad
Philippines	maintain	maintain	maintain	may vote abroad
Poland	maintain	maintain	no intervention	may vote abroad
Portugal	maintain	maintain	maintain	may vote abroad*
Puerto Rico	–	–	–	–
Qatar	lower	maintain	no intervention	no elections
Romania	lower	no intervention	lower	may vote abroad
Russia	raise	raise	no intervention	may vote abroad

* may vote in legislative elections for special representative for people living outside country

United Nations instruments				
Date of ratification as of *July 2009*				
1951 Refugee Convention	1967 Refugee Protocol	1990 Migrant Workers Convention	2000 Human Trafficking Protocol	
–	–	–	2005	Lebanon
1981	1981	2005	2003	Lesotho
1964	1980	–	2004	Liberia
–	–	2004	2004	Libya
1997	1997	–	2003	Lithuania
1953	1971	–	2009	Luxembourg
1994	1994	–	2005	Macedonia
1967	–	–	2005	Madagascar
1987	1987	–	2005	Malawi
–	–	–	2009	Malaysia
–	–	–	–	Maldives
1973	1973	2003	2002	Mali
1971	1971	–	2003	Malta
–	–	–	–	Marshall Islands
1987	1987	2007	2005	Mauritania
–	–	–	2003	Mauritius
2000	2000	1999	2003	Mexico
–	–	–	–	Micronesia, Fed. Sts.
2002	2002	–	2005	Moldova
–	–	–	2008	Mongolia
2006	2006	–	2006	Montenegro
1956	1971	1993	–	Morocco
1983	1989	–	2006	Mozambique
1995	1995	–	2002	Namibia
–	–	–	–	Nauru
–	–	–	–	Nepal
1956	1968	–	2005	Netherlands
1960	1973	–	2002	New Zealand
1980	1980	2005	2004	Nicaragua
1961	1970	2009	2004	Niger
1967	1968	–	2001	Nigeria
-	-	-	-	Niue
1953	1967	–	2003	Norway
–	–	–	2005	Oman
–	–	–	–	Pakistan
–	–	–	–	Palau
-	-	-	-	Palestinian Territories
1978	1978	–	2004	Panama
1986	1986	–	–	Papua New Guinea
1970	1970	2008	2004	Paraguay
1964	1983	2005	2002	Peru
1981	1981	1995	2002	Philippines
1991	1991	–	2003	Poland
1960	1976	–	2004	Portugal
-	-	-	-	Puerto Rico
–	–	–	2009	Qatar
1991	1991	–	2002	Romania
1993	1993	–	2004	Russia

MIGRATION POLICY

	Government policy			Voting status of people living abroad in relation to elections in country of origin 2009	
	on level of immigration 2005	on highly skilled immigrants 2005	on emigration 2005		
Rwanda	maintain	no intervention	maintain	may vote abroad	
St. Kitts & Nevis	maintain	maintain	no intervention	cannot vote	
St. Lucia	maintain	maintain	no intervention	cannot vote	
St. Vincent & Grenadines	maintain	maintain	no intervention	must return to vote	
Samoa	maintain	maintain	maintain	no data	
São Tomé & Principe	no intervention	–	no intervention	may vote abroad	
Saudi Arabia	lower	lower	lower	no elections	
Senegal	no intervention	–	no intervention	may vote abroad	
Serbia	maintain	raise	lower	must return to vote	
Seychelles	maintain	–	maintain	cannot vote	
Sierra Leone	no intervention	–	no intervention	cannot vote	
Singapore	raise	raise	lower	may vote abroad	
Slovakia	maintain	maintain	no intervention	must return to vote	
Slovenia	maintain	maintain	no intervention	may vote abroad	
Solomon Islands	maintain	maintain	maintain	must return to vote	
Somalia	–	–	–	no elections	
South Africa	lower	maintain	lower	may vote abroad	
Spain	maintain	maintain	lower	may vote abroad	
Sri Lanka	maintain	maintain	maintain	cannot vote	
Sudan	maintain	–	lower	may vote abroad	
Suriname	raise	raise	lower	cannot vote	
Swaziland	maintain	–	no intervention	no data	
Sweden	maintain	maintain	no intervention	may vote abroad	
Switzerland	maintain	raise	no intervention	may vote abroad	
Syria	maintain	–	lower	may vote abroad	
Tajikistan	maintain	–	no intervention	may vote abroad	
Tanzania	no intervention	–	no intervention	cannot vote	
Thailand	maintain	maintain	raise	may vote abroad	
Togo	no intervention	no intervention	no intervention	may vote abroad	
Tonga	maintain	maintain	maintain	must return to vote	
Trinidad & Tobago	maintain	maintain	no intervention	cannot vote	
Tunisia	no intervention	no intervention	raise	may vote abroad	
Turkey	lower	raise	maintain	may vote abroad	
Turkmenistan	lower	–	lower	no data	
Tuvalu	maintain	–	raise	no data	
Uganda	maintain	–	no intervention	cannot vote	
Ukraine	maintain	maintain	lower	may vote abroad	
United Arab Emirates	lower	lower	no intervention	no elections	
United Kingdom	maintain	raise	no intervention	may vote abroad	
United States	maintain	maintain	no intervention	may vote abroad	
Uruguay	maintain	maintain	no intervention	no data	
Uzbekistan	maintain	maintain	maintain	may vote abroad	
Vanuatu	no intervention	–	no intervention	may vote abroad	
Venezuela	maintain	maintain	no intervention	may vote abroad	
Vietnam	maintain	maintain	raise	no data	
Yemen	lower	maintain	raise	may vote abroad	
Zambia	raise	maintain	lower	no data	
Zimbabwe	no intervention	raise	lower	cannot vote	

* may vote in legislative elections for special representative for people living outside country

United Nations instruments Date of ratification as of *July 2009*				
1951 Refugee Convention	1967 Refugee Protocol	1990 Migrant Workers Convention	2000 Human Trafficking Protocol	
1980	1980	2008	2003	Rwanda
2002	–	–	2004	St. Kitts & Nevis
–	–	–	–	St. Lucia
1993	2003	–	–	St. Vincent & Grenadines
1988	1994	–	–	Samoa
1978	1978	–	2006	São Tomé & Principe
–	–	–	2007	Saudi Arabia
1963	1967	1999	2003	Senegal
2001	2001	–	2001	Serbia
1980	1980	1994	2004	Seychelles
1981	1981	–	–	Sierra Leone
–	–	–	–	Singapore
1993	1993	–	2004	Slovakia
1992	1992	–	2004	Slovenia
1995	1995	–	–	Solomon Islands
1978	1978	–	–	Somalia
1996	1996	–	2004	South Africa
1978	1978	–	2002	Spain
–	–	1996	–	Sri Lanka
1974	1974	–	–	Sudan
1978	1978	–	2007	Suriname
2000	1969	–	–	Swaziland
1954	1967	–	2004	Sweden
1955	1968	–	2006	Switzerland
–	–	2005	2009	Syria
1993	1993	2002	2002	Tajikistan
1964	1968	–	2006	Tanzania
–	–	–	–	Thailand
1962	1969	–	2009	Togo
–	–	–	–	Tonga
2000	2000	–	2007	Trinidad & Tobago
1957	1968	–	2003	Tunisia
1962	1968	2004	2003	Turkey
1998	1998	–	2005	Turkmenistan
1986	1986	–	–	Tuvalu
1976	1976	1995	–	Uganda
2002	2002	–	2004	Ukraine
–	–	–	2009	United Arab Emirates
1954	1968	–	2006	United Kingdom
–	1968	–	2005	United States
1970	1970	2001	2005	Uruguay
–	–	–	2008	Uzbekistan
–	–	–	–	Vanuatu
–	1986	–	2002	Venezuela
–	–	–	–	Vietnam
1980	1980	–	–	Yemen
1969	1969	–	2005	Zambia
1981	1981	–	–	Zimbabwe

SOURCES

For sources available on the internet, in most cases only the root address has been given. To view the source, it is recommended that the reader type the title of the page or document into Google or another search engine.

Please note that the rounding of data for presentation in some graphics has resulted in the segments in some pie charts not totalling 100 percent.

PART ONE: THE GRAND NARRATIVE

20–21 EARLY MIGRATIONS
National Geographic: The Genographic Project https://genographic.nationalgeographic.com
Scotese CR. Paleomar Project. www.scotese.com

22–23 MEDITERRANEAN ODYSSEYS
Greek and Phoenician Colonial Migrations
L'atlas des migrations. Paris: Le Monde Hors-Serie; 2008-09. p.18-19.
King R. editor. *The history of human migration*. London: New Holland; 2007. p.50-51.

The Growth of the Roman Empire
King R. 2007. op. cit.

24–25 SLAVE MIGRATIONS
Trade in People
Curtin PD. *The Atlantic slave trade: a census*. Madison: University of Wisconsin Press; 1969. p.268.

Slave Trade
Potts L. *The world labour market: a history of migration*. London: Zed Books; 1990. p.42.
Segal A. *An atlas of international migration*. London: Zell; 1993. p.55.

26–27 MIGRATIONS OF INDENTURE
King R. Migration in a world historical perspective. In: van den Broeck J. editor. *The economics of labour migration*. Cheltenham: Edward Elgar; 1996. pp.7-75.
Potts L. *The world labour market: a history of migration*. London: Zed Books; 1990. pp.72, 76–7, 85-88.

28–29 THE GREAT MIGRATION
Baines D. *Emigration from Europe 1815-1930*. London: Macmillan; 1991.
Gabaccia D. *Italy's many diasporas*. London: UCL Press; 2000.
Piore MJ. *Birds of passage: migrant labor in industrial societies*. New York: Cambridge University Press; 1979.

European Emigration
Baines. 1991. op. cit.

Long-Distance Migrations
Baines. 1991. op. cit.
Segal A. *An atlas of international migration*. London: Zell; 1993. pp.16-17.

30–31 MIGRATION FROM ITALY
Rosoli G. editor. *Un secolo di emigrazione Italiana: 1876-1976*. Rome: Centro Studi Emigrazione; 1978.

32–33 NATION-BUILDING MIGRATIONS
Settlement of USA
O'Brien PK. editor. Philip's atlas of world history. London: Philip's. New York: Oxford University Press; 1999. p.183.

Planned Migration
Tirtosudarmo R. Mobility and human development in Indonesia. Human Development Research Paper 2009/19. UNDP; 2009. Table 2.2.

34–35 COLONIAL MIGRATIONS
Ethnic Composition
CIA. The World Factbook. www.cia.gov.uk

European Empires
Cohen R. editor. *Cambridge survey of world migration*. Cambridge University Press; 1995.

36–37 DIASPORAS
Jews Living in Israel
Robert Schumann Centre for Advanced Studies. www.carim.org

Jewish Migration to Israel
L'atlas des migrations. Paris: Le Monde Hors-Serie; 2008-09. p.93.
Robert Schumann Centre for Advanced Studies. www.carim.org
Central Bureau of Statistics (Israel), Statistical Abstract of Israel 2008. Citing primary source as: Division
   of Jewish Demography and Statistics. The A. Harman Institute of Contemporary Jewry. The Hebrew
   University of Jerusalem.

Greek Diaspora
Figures downloaded from General Secretariat for Greeks Abroad www.ggae.gr/gabroad/organosi.en.asp

Lebanese Diaspora
Lebanese Emigration Research Center (LERC) at Notre Dame University-Louaizé, Lebanon.
Simon G. *La Planete Migratoire dans la Mondialisation*. Paris: Armand Colin; 2008.

PART TWO: A WORLD IN FLUX

40–41 GLOBAL MIGRATION
United Nations Population Division Department of Economic and Social Affairs. International Migration
   2009. www.un.org/esa/population/unpop.htm

42–43 POST-WAR MIGRATION OF WORKERS
Population Movements in Japan
Japanese Census data. www.stat.go.jp/english/data/idou/1.htm

Labour Migration in Europe
Hammar T. editor. *European immigration policy: a comparative study*. Cambridge: Cambridge University
   Press; 1985.
King RL. Migration. In: Clout H et al. editors. *Western Europe: geographical perspectives*. London:
   Longman (2nd ed); 1989. pp. 40-60.

44–45 NEW WORKER MIGRATIONS
United Nations Global Migration Database v.0.3.6 http://esa.un.org/unmigration

46–47 THE QUIET MIGRATION
Major Inflows of Relatives to the UK
Dependants in the UK
Control of Immigration: Statistics UK 2008 Table 4C. Home Office; 2009. www.homeoffice.gov.uk

48–49 LATIN AMERICA
Growing Number of Hispanics in the USA
US Census Bureau www.census.gov
Major Population Movements
15 million more people...
Global Migrant Origin Database. Updated March 2007 - Version 4, Migration DRC. www.nsd.uib.no

50–51 THE GULF
A Rapidly Increasing Migrant Workforce
UN Pop Division http://esa.un.org/migration/index.asp?panel=1

Migrants to the Gulf
United Nations Population Division Department of Economic and Social Affairs. International Migration 2009.
Kapiszewski A. Arab versus Asian migrant workers in the GCC countries. United Nations Population Division Department of Economic and Social Affairs. 2006 May 22.

52–53 PATTERNS OF MIGRATION IN EURASIA
Ethnic Origins
International Organization for Migration. Migration in the Russian Federation: a country profile 2008. Table 14. http://publications.iom.int

Migration Towards and Within Russia
Ivakhnyuk I. The Russian migration policy and its impact. 2009 UNDP Human Development Research Paper 2009/14.
The 2002 Russian Census www.perepis2002.ru
Gerber TP. Regional economic performance and net migration rates in Russia, 1993-2002. *International Migration Review* 2006;40(3): 661-97.
International Organization for Migration. Migration in the Russian Federation: a country profile 2008. http://publications.iom.int

More than 10%...
The 2002 Russian Census.

54–55 MIGRATION WITHIN INDIA
Movement of people: Census of India www.censusindia.gov.in
GSDP per capita. Annexure VIIIB. State-wise per capita income at current prices; 2008 Jan 31. Department of Planning, Government of Punjab. www.pbplanning.gov.in
Mumbai GDP per capita. Economic survey of Maharashtra. 2004–05. p.164. www.maharashtra.gov.in

56–57 MIGRATION WITHIN THE USA
Reasons Given for Migration
Bogue, DJ. et al. *Immigration, internal migration and local mobility in the US*. Edward Elgar; 2009.

Trends in Internal Migration
Internal Migration in the USA
US Census Bureau. www.census.gov

58–59 INTERNAL MIGRATION & POVERTY
Internal Migration in Ghana
Level of Education
2000 Ghana Census.

Internal Migration in China
GDP: *China statistical yearbook 2007*. Beijing: China Statistics Press; 2007.
Flows of people: 2005 1% Population Survey Data Assembly. Chinadataonline.org. Courtesy Bao Shuming, University of Michigan.

Type of Employment
Education of Migrants
Level of Education
Communiqué on major data of the Second National Agricultural Census of China no.5. www.stats.gov.cn

PART THREE: THE AGE OF MIGRATION

62–63 REFUGEES
UNHCR Statistics www.unhcr.org [Accessed 2009 October].
UNHCR Statistical yearbooks 1993–98.

64–65 REFUGEE WAREHOUSING
UNHCR Statistics www.unhcr.org

UNRWA www.un.org/unrwa/english.html

66–67 REFUGEE RETURN
UNHCR Statistical yearbooks.

68–69 SEEKING ASYLUM IN EUROPE
UNHCR Statistics www.unhcr.org
Eurostat http://epp.eurostat.ec.europa.eu/portal/page/portal/eurostat/home

70–71 INTERNALLY DISPLACED PERSONS
Internally Displaced Persons
IDMC. Internal displacement: global overview of trends and development in 2008. p.4.
www.internal-displacement.org

Colombia
IDMC 2008. op. cit. p.91.

Philippines
IDMC 2008. op. cit. p.65.

Photo captions
Panos Photos. www.panos.co.uk
1.27 million displaced by China's Three Gorges Dam. 2009, Sept 13. Report from Beijing AFP.
http://chinhdangvu.blogspot.com

72–73 CLIMATE CHANGE
Impact of Hurricane Katrina
US Census Bureau. www.census.gov

Vulnerable Deltas
IPCC. Fourth assessment report. Climate change 2007: Working Group II: Impacts, adaption and
vulnerability. 6.5.1.2 Deltas. Box 6.3. Figure 6.6.

Photo caption
Gommes R, du Guerny J, Nachtergaele F, Brinkman R. Potential impacts of sea-level rise on populations
and agriculture. Food and Agriculture Organization; 1998 Mar. www.fao.org/sd/eidirect/eire0047.htm

74–75 IRREGULAR MIGRATION
Major Irregular Border Crossings
US Department of Homeland Security www.dhs.gov/index.shtm
European Agency for the Management of Operational Cooperation at the External Borders (FRONTEX)
http://europa.eu/agencies/community_agencies/frontex/index_en.htm

Trafficking
Map colour: Trafficking in persons report 2009. US Department of State. Washington DC. www.state.gov
Arrows: various sources.

76–77 DEATH AT THE BORDER
Cause of Death
European Border Deaths
Platform for International Cooperation on Undocumented Migration www.picum.org

US–Mexico Border Deaths
Jimenez M. *Humanitarian crisis: migrant deaths at the US Mexico border*, San Diego: ACLU and Mexico's
National Commission on Human Rights; 2009.

Photo caption
Robbins T. San Diego fence provides lesson in border control. 2006 Apr 6. www.npr.org

78–79 Migration & Gender
Origin and Gender of Migrants from Philippines
National Statistical Office: 2007 and 2008 Survey on Overseas Filipinos. www.census.gov.ph

Filipinos Abroad
Commission on Filipinos Overseas. Stock estimate of overseas Filipinos. As of December 2007. www.cfo.gov.ph
Philippine Overseas Employment Administration. OFW Deployment per country and skill Jan 01, 2006 to Dec 31, 2006. www.poea.gov.ph

80–81 Migration for Marriage
Korean Population Census 2005.
Korean Immigration Service 2009.

82–83 Child Migration
Independent Child Migrants
Yaqub S. Child migrants with and without parents: census-based estimates of scale and characteristics in Argentina, Chile and South Africa. UNICEF Innocenti Research Centre. Discussion paper no. 2009-02. 2009 Feb. p.13.

International Child Migration
IPUMS International.

Young Migrants in Ghana
Age at First Migration
Occupation
Kwankye SO, Anarfi JK, Tagoe CA. and Castaldo A. Working Paper T-29. Independent north–south child migration in Ghana: the decision making process. 2009 Feb. Development Research Centre on Migration, Globalisation and Poverty. University of Sussex, UK. Source of data is a survey of under 24-year olds working in markets in Accra and Kumasi, carried out by the Institute for Statistical, Social and Economic Research (ISSER) at the University of Ghana, Legon, in 2005.

84–85 Student Migration
Origins
Destinations
Major Student Flows
Global education digest 2008. Paris: UNESCO. www.uis.unesco.org
Open Doors. New York: Institute of International Education; 2008. www.opendoors.iienetwork.org
Student mobility, internationalization of higher education and skilled migration. In: *World migration 2008*. Geneva: International Organization for Migration; 2008. pp.105-125.

86–87 Skilled Migration
Docquier F, Marfouk A. International migration by education attainment. 1990-2000. In:. Özden Ç, Schiff M. editors. *International migration, remittances and the brain drain.* Washington: The World Bank; 2006. pp.151-199.
OECD online database. stats.oecd.org

88–89 International Retirement
Pensioners Abroad
UK Department for Work and Pensions Information Directorate: Work and pensions longitudinal study.

Foreign Pensioners in Spain
Population and Housing Census 2001. www.ine.es/censo/en/listatablas.jsp

90–91 Return Migration
Country Policies on Return Migration
United Nations. Department of Economic and Social Affairs. Population Division. International Migration 2006.

Italian Migrants
Rate of Return to Italy
King R. Patterns of Italian migrant labour: the historical and geographical context. University of Bristol. Centre for Mediterranean Studies. Occasional Paper no. 4. 1992. p.23.

92–93 MIGRATION & INTEGRATION
Migrant Integration Policy Index (MIPEX) www.integrationindex.eu/mapscharts

94–95 VOTING FROM ABROAD
Collyer M, Vathi Z. Patterns of extra-territorial voting. Working paper T22. Sussex Centre for Migration Research; Oct 2007.

96–97 DUAL NATIONALITY
Howard MM. Variation in dual citizenship policies in the countries of the EU. *International Migration Review*; 2005. 39(3) 697-720.
US Office of Personnel Management. Citizenship laws of the world. US Office of Personnel Management: Washington DC; 2001.
Dual citizenship. www.citizenship.gov.au/current/dual_citizenship

98–99 REMITTANCES & DEVELOPMENT
Remittances
United Nations, Department of Economic and Social Affairs, Population Division, International Migration 2009. www.unmigration.org

Average Remittances
The World Bank. Data & Research. http://econ.worldbank.org
World Development Indicators. www.wri.org

100–01 MIGRATION POLICY
UN Department of Economic and Social Affairs Population Division. International Migration 2006. October 2006. www.un.org/esa/population/publications/2006Migration_Chart

TABLE: ECONOMICS & MOVEMENT
Population, GDP: World Development Indicators online database.
Remittances, Migrants, Net Migration: United Nations, Department of Economic and Social Affairs, Population Division, International Migration 2009. www.unmigration.org
Refugees, Total population of concern: UNHCR 2008 Global Trends. 2009 June 10.
IDPs: IDMC. Internal displacement: global overview of trends and development in 2008.

TABLE: MIGRATION POLICY
Government policy: United Nations, Department of Economic and Social Affairs, Population Division, International Migration 2006.
Voting status: Collyer M, Vathi Z. Patterns of extra-territorial voting. Working paper T22. Sussex Centre for Migration Research; 2007 Oct.
United Nations instruments: United Nations, Department of Economic and Social Affairs, Population Division, International Migration 2009.

INDEX